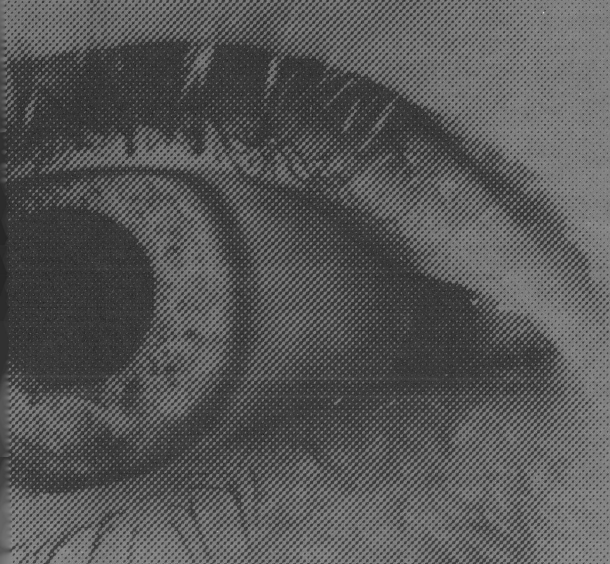

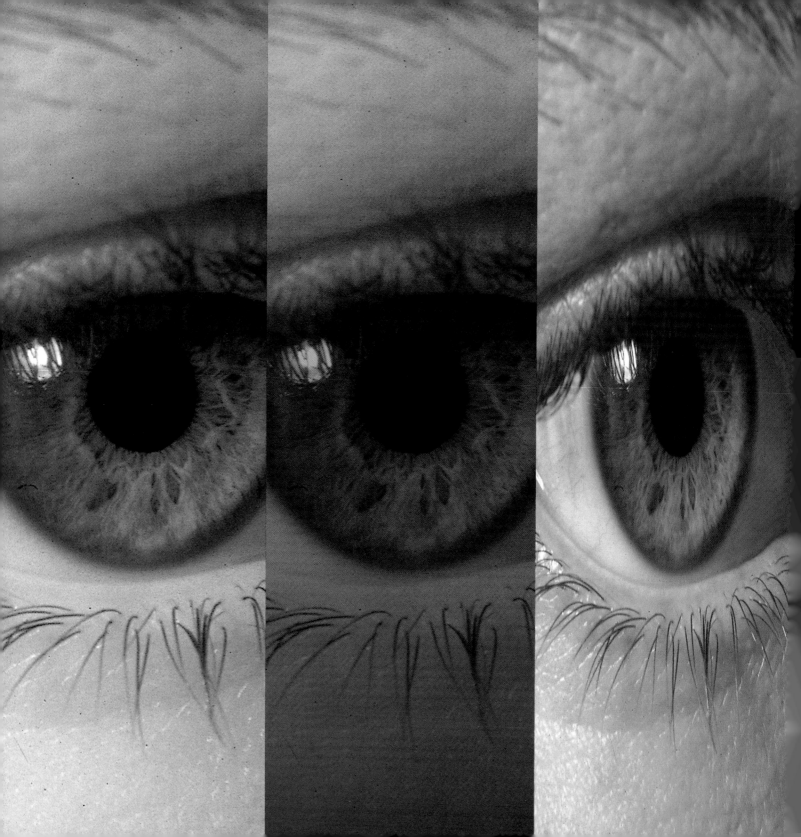

HALFTONE EFFECTS

PETER BRIDGEWATER

AND GERALD WOODS

CHRONICLE BOOKS

SAN FRANCISCO

First published in the United States in 1993 by Chronicle Books.
Copyright © 1992 Quarto Publishing plc

All rights reserved. No part of this book may be reproduced, without written permission of the Publisher.

Library of Congress Cataloging in Publication Data available.

ISBN 0-8118-0311-2

Distributed in Canada by
Raincoast Books
112 East Third Avenue
Vancouver, B.C.
V5T 1C8

Published by
Chronicle Books
275 Fifth Street
San Francisco
California 94103

A QUARTO BOOK

This book was designed and produced by Quarto Publishing plc,
The Old Brewery, 6 Blundell Street, London N7 9BH

10 9 8 7 6 5 4 3 2 1

Typeset by CST, Eastbourne/Peter Bridgewater Ltd
Manufactured in Singapore by Colour Trend Singapore
Printed in Singapore by Star Standard Industries (Pte.) Ltd

Design: Peter Bridgewater
Consultant: Moira Clinch
Photographer: Jeremy Thomas
Picture Research: Vivian Adleman
Picture Manager: Rebecca Horsewood
Senior Editor: Kate Kirby
Editor: Louise Bostock
Production Director: Richard Neo

Art Director: Moira Clinch
Publishing Director: Janet Slingsby

The images in this book have been proofed to the highest possible standards. However, it should be remembered that color origination depends on the reproduction techniques involved and the paper used.

You should always ask for trial proofs if you are trying to match a technique.

This book contains examples of graphic design work. These examples are included for the purpose of criticism and review.

With special thanks to Wilfred Tan at Colour Trend Singapore for technical support during reproduction, and to the team at Colour Trend Singapore for creating the special halftone effects used in this book; to Bournemouth Colour Graphics for images on pp132–137

Contents

SECTION ONE

WORKING WITH TWO COLOR

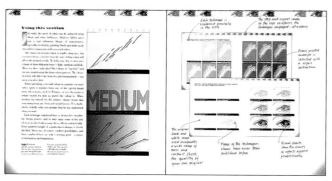

WORKING WITH FOUR COLOR

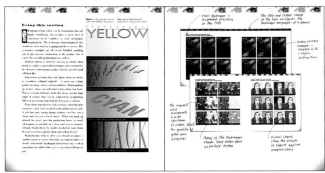

SECTION THREE

SPECIAL EFFECTS

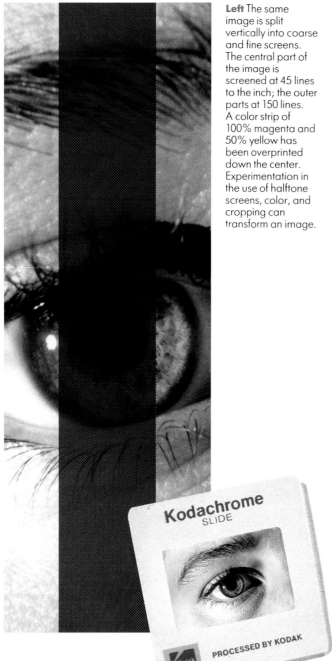

Left The same image is split vertically into coarse and fine screens. The central part of the image is screened at 45 lines to the inch; the outer parts at 150 lines. A color strip of 100% magenta and 50% yellow has been overprinted down the center. Experimentation in the use of halftone screens, color, and cropping can transform an image.

INTRODUCTION

The greater mastery a designer has over technique, the more closely he or she will be able to match the final printed work with the original design concept. The kind of proficiency this requires can only come through day-to-day working experience and professional practice. But in the use of halftone processes, even the most experienced designer often takes a risk over the look of the end product. Specifying these techniques is usually a visual gamble.

To the novice, the technical aspects of reproduction processes can seem extremely daunting in their complexity. And as with most professions, graphic design has its own jargon that needs to be understood in order to obtain the required results from printers and process technicians. There is, however, no need for anxiety. Always ask a printer or color separation house to explain anything you do not understand, and never be afraid to admit a lack of technical knowledge and ask for help. Much can also be achieved by following the simple procedures demonstrated in this book. However, do not try to encompass the whole range of techniques at once.

The kind of techniques you need to be conversant with are determined by the nature of the problem you are handling. In other words, use techniques as you need them. In that way you will tend to learn about them more easily and with greater understanding. As you gain confidence you will find your own way of approaching a new task. Remember that for all of us, the learning process never ends. We all continually go on adding to our existing store of knowledge. Whether you are designing a book

Below A trained operator, working from an art director's brief, uses a Quantel Graphic Paintbox. This system makes possible the full combination of electronically manipulated images.

Below right A "grabbed" image, produced by manipulating and distorting the original through the Quantel system.

jacket, a press advertisement, or a piece of packaging, every element in your design should be there for a purpose – special halftone effects that are superfluous to the essential design or essential mood could be detrimental to the work as a whole. Used effectively, on the other hand, halftone techniques can enhance a design.

The increasing sophistication of computer technology means that designers now have more immediate access to a wide range of effects. They can also gain hands-on experience more readily. But there are inherent dangers; such tools can be used in the wrong way by designers with insufficient visual training or technical competence. An inexperienced operator might, for instance, use the wrong screen angles when producing a full-color image by computer. The point to be made is that while one welcomes advances in image-making technology, a machine cannot provide a substitute for a good design sense. Computer technology cannot disguise bad design.

Top The dark and uneven background tones of the original are removed by cutting out around the contours. A lighter solid tint lends greater emphasis to the figure.

What is a halftone?

A halftone is a means of breaking up the continuous solid tone of an original image into a great many tiny individual dots of varying sizes. The closer and larger the dot, the darker the image area. When printed, the illusion of a smooth gradation of value from light to dark is created. In general, the human eye does not distinguish the small dots that constitute a photographic reproduction in a newspaper or magazine. When magnified, however, the screen can be seen distinctly, and it is also possible to see that the size of the dot determines the tonal values of the picture. All the main printing processes – photolithography, gravure, and silkscreen (serigraphy) – require an image to be broken down into printing and non-printing areas in this way. Only with the Collotype process is it possible to produce fine gradations of tone without a screen. Collotype is a printing process which uses glycerin. It is very expensive and rarely used.

Traditionally, when an original is to be produced by halftone, the process technician places a glass screen ruled with a rectangular grid of fine diagonal lines between the original and the negative. The screen breaks up the original into cones of light, which form the diagonal pattern of dots of various sizes to compose the conventional halftone. The pattern of dots must be diagonal in order to be inconspicuous.

In addition to glass screens, contact screens are sometimes used. These are made up of vignetted dots and placed directly in contact with the unexposed film.

Above Generally the eye does not see the halftone dot. It becomes distinct only when seen through a magnifying glass.

Top right The dot pattern of the halftone is seen clearly in the magnified lower-right part of the image.

Above The screen angles of this image have been incorrectly aligned during the origination stage. Notice how the dots (aligned vertically) become far more conspicuous when the wrong angle is selected.

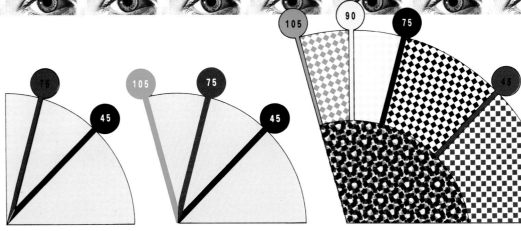

In order to avoid moiré, it is critical that correct screen angles are used. **Above** When an image is being printed in two colors, the black screen is placed at 45° – the second color at 75°.

Above The screen angles of 45° and 75° are also used in three-color printing with the third color angled at 105°.

Above In four-color printing, the black screen is angled at 45°, magenta at 75°, the cyan screen at 105°, and yellow at 90°.

Above A conventional glass screen has been used to produce this image.

Above The same image made from a negative produced on an electronic scanner. Notice how much more detail is achieved.

Computerized electronic scanning is increasingly replacing the conventional processes just described. The original artwork or transparency is taped to the cylindrical drum of the laser scanner. So if your color separator is using a scanner the artwork will need to be flexible.

The technician operating the scanner can pre-set the screen ruling and any percentage enlargement or reduction that might be necessary. As the drum rotates at high speed, the scanning head reads the image while it moves along the drum. Signals received through color-filtration are converted by the computer to produce a screened separated image on film. Scanners are also used for black and white halftones, primarily because a laser can break up a halftone into more than 200 modulations of the gray tones.

The resulting image is therefore superior in every way to the conventional halftone screen, which is always subject to scratches, dust, or a lens being out of focus.

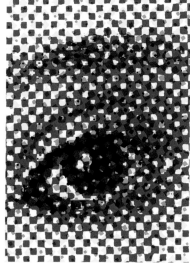

Screens

The gauge of the screen ruling determines the frequency of dots, usually described in lines to the inch. For instance, newspapers are printed at very high speeds on fairly rough paper. Therefore a coarse screen of 45–80 lines to the inch would be most suitable. Finer screens of 120 lines to the inch upward require smoother paper of good quality. Where high definition is required, for example in photographic books, a very fine screen of 200 or even 300 lines to the inch might be used, with a high-quality coated paper. When selecting a paper for a particular job, it is always worth asking the printer to evaluate its suitability.

Right The same image is reproduced here using different screen sizes. Clockwise from top left: 50 lines per inch, 75 lines per inch, 100 lines per inch, 150 lines per inch.

Above When enlarged, the overlapping dots of a four-color halftone become "Pop Art" in their effect.

Right The shape of the halftone dot varies according to the method of reproduction. Conventional dot shapes produced by a contact screen are square. A scanner can produce a range of dot shapes — round or elliptical, for example — which makes possible a greater range of tone and finer definition.

Above A fine screen printed on a coated paper. Because coated papers are less absorbent than newsprint or drawing paper, the dots are less likely to spread, and the image is much sharper.

Above Newsprint is very absorbent. If too fine a screen is used (here it is 150°), the ink tends to bleed, and dots join together forming a solid layer of ink and a consequent loss of detail.

Above Here the image is printed on newsprint using a coarse screen (65-85 lines per inch). There is some loss of density, but the image is nevertheless sharper.

Paper

The color, tone, and texture of the paper can be critical to the quality of the printed image. A white paper reflects any color that is printed on it. But while colored papers can be used very effectively in design, they are subject to absorption. For instance, if blue is printed on yellow paper, it will be absorbed, but the same yellow paper reflects red and green. Magenta absorbs green because the two colors are complementary, but magenta reflects red and blue. Black absorbs all colors.

The textural quality of the paper depends on the constituents used in its manufacture and the machine finish. High-quality halftones should be printed on a coated paper in order to obtain a perfectly sharp image. The coating used on such papers contains china clay for extra smoothness. Imitation coated papers can be polished or matte, and the china clay is mixed with the wood pulp. Fluorescing agents are sometimes added during the manufacturing process to increase the overall whiteness of the paper. Some paper manufacturers provide samples of the way that halftones will appear on different stock.

For the proofing of halftones, a specialized paper is generally used. This is very smooth, and it is coated on one side only. For general book and magazine production, a woodfree paper is used. Packaging, labels, and some booklets all require special coated papers, which are machine polished.

Special screens

In addition to conventional screens, there are a number of special effect screens that can be used by the designer. A one-way screen has lines that are ruled in one direction – the lines are thin for lighter tones, and increase in thickness for darker tones. A photographic image that is sliced up in this way has the effect of conveying a sense of movement. A one-way screen can be used to advantage in architectural or industrial subjects, where the linear pattern enhances the structural aspect of the original. A curved one-way screen is sometimes used to emphasize volume and form, for example in portraiture.

The linen screen renders an image that is broken up by a coarse cloth-like texture. This has a variety of creative applications, most especially where a photographic image needs to be given the appearance of a painting on canvas.

The Erwin (or mezzotint) screen is named after a traditional etching technique which renders soft tones. The fine granular quality it produces can convey a strong sense of atmosphere. All of these screens can, of course, be produced in a range of percentages of strength in the same way as a halftone screen.

Left The design of this magazine cover demonstrates how halftone screens, combined with type and color, can be used creatively.

Below A textured screen – in this case a cross-hatched screen – creates the effect of a pen-and-ink sketch.

Right A horizontal line screen has been employed to break up this image of the running feet of an athlete, creating a strong sense of movement and speed.

Duotones and tritones

A true duotone is achieved by printing two halftone films of the same original together in two different colors. In the duotone process, two halftone negatives (and therefore two halftone plates) are made, each with a different screen angle. Usually, one film is exposed to register the highlights of the image, and the other to bring out the darker tones. When printed in register, the effect of a high definition photograph is created, and this gives the image on the page a "lift." For this reason, the duotone is often employed where the quality of the photographic image is critical. If a black tint is used for one plate and a colored ink for the second, it is possible to create a specific mood or atmosphere that is perhaps not present in the original. If, for example, the designer has an original photograph of, say, cows grazing by a riverbank, the image as it stands may not be especially poignant. If, however, a duotone in black and sepia is created, the nostalgic atmosphere of early landscape photography can be evoked. Using colors and tints not normally associated with a subject can produce a slightly surreal or dreamlike quality in the picture.

Sometimes a black and white halftone printed in black over a flat tint of a second color can be mistaken for a duotone. This technique, although effective, will result in less depth and detail than a true duotone.

In the search for even finer image definition, a third color is sometimes added to create a tritone. The third tone is often gray or sepia to give even greater depth and more detail.

Right An example of a mezzotint screen. The granular chalk-like quality softens the image so that it looks more like a drawing than a photograph. A color tint of 30% cyan and 10% yellow is laid to highlight the marble.

Below A composite image made up of a halftone (top), duotone (middle), and tritone (bottom).

What is a fifth color?

When designing for book or magazine production, continuity of color is important. Problems might arise, however, when the color specified for a sequence of pages cannot be maintained. This occurs because, with four-color reproduction, the strength and tone of a tint is influenced by the weight of the same color on different pages. When printing a section of pages, the density of the ink fed into the offset lithography machine is adjusted to get the best out of the various images. This means that any color made from mixing percentage tints together from the four process colors will vary from section to section. If, for example, a border tint of blue is required to run through a sequence of pages, the density of that blue may change during printing. A fifth color would need to be introduced in order to maintain accurate color continuity throughout. This will, of course, increase production costs, and may not be possible or even necessary.

Right This shows special PANTONE colors and their equivalents made up using tints of the four process colors. The four-color process cannot match the quality and range that PANTONE offers.

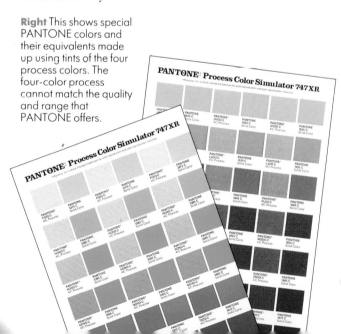

Pantone Matching System®

The PANTONE MATCHING SYSTEM, which has now been in use for several decades, was originally developed to bring some kind of order to color-matching. Previously, designers simply attached cut or torn color samples from various sources to the artwork, in the vague hope that the printer would be able to match the sample with printing inks. This inevitably meant that the printer spent a great deal of time mixing colors, and this pushed up production costs. The results were often unsatisfactory, both for the designer and for the client.

The PANTONE Color Formula Guide contained the formulas for various color combinations, and could be used by both designer and printer alike. As the system evolved, a book with tear-out color samples was introduced, which could be used by the designer to attach directly to the artwork. For design visuals, a set of coordinating felt marker pens, adhesive films, and colored paper was also introduced, so that from the outset, the designer could use color that would match the final printed image.

In recent years, the Pantone company has greatly extended its color range from the initial 500 colors. It now includes warm and cool grays, bright primary colors, and even fluorescent color inks.

The PANTONE MATCHING SYSTEM is used throughout the world. It is a system which allows designers, clients and printers to communicate in a reliable way when specifying colors.

PANTONE MATCHING SYSTEM® is a registered trademark of Pantone, Inc.

Checking originals

It cannot be emphasized too strongly that the quality of all photographs reproduced by the halftone process depends entirely on the quality of the original. No printing process, however refined, can compensate for a sloppy original. While a good process technician might well be able to enhance part of an image, it is usually at the expense of a tone elsewhere. For example, if lighter tones are heightened, the blacks could at the same time lose some of their density. As a general rule, originals that are reduced rather than enlarged tend to be sharper in reproduction.

It is virtually impossible to match the exact qualities of the original with a halftone reproduction of the same image – the tone of the photograph is denser and continuous. A photograph reproduced and printed by offset lithography, for instance, often seems gray in comparison with the original. Therefore, all original photographs should have sharply contrasting tones. The best results are obtained when the original image has a well-defined scale of grays, rather than soft tones that merge into one another. To sum up, the photograph should have sharp focus and a modulation of tone from white to black.

Other forms of original artwork need to be checked for indentations, cracking or peeling designer's color, and any unwanted surface marks. Remember, never use paper-clips on halftone originals as the scanner will pick up the impression and you will find it reproduced on the job. If the original is going to be scanned, it will have to be wrapped around a drum. It is much easier, if this is the case, for the artwork to be on a flexible board.

Above The original on the left is unsuitable for reproduction – the tonal balance is incorrect. The image on the right is well-balanced for reproduction, and the print is undamaged.

Below When checking the suitability of transparencies for reproduction, make sure that the image is sharp and free from scratches, dust, or any extraneous marks.

Creative applications

When first visualizing any design concept, the designer is faced with the task of using every technique at his or her disposal to arrest the attention of the potential audience. Whether trying to convey a subtle psychological message on behalf of a client, or helping to sell a car, the essential task is to create a design that will be noticed and therefore be effective. In a society that has become saturated with imagery from a great many sources, it has become all the more difficult to design a book, magazine, package, or any form of publicity that will arouse sufficient interest to make people pause for even a second.

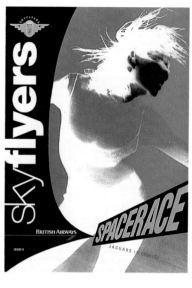

Left In this creative collage of images, the enlarged halftone dot is used as an essential part of the graphic statement.

The magazine and book designer, for example, is rarely concerned with static images – in these disciplines, the sequential aspect of design is important. For instance, a well-designed magazine offers the reader a series of visual surprises from one page to the next. The astute use of halftone techniques can distinguish lively magazines from their less imaginative competitors. On one double

spread in such a publication, one might find halftones that are squared, silhouetted, vignetted, fed through a fax, or ghosted, and printed with coarse and fine screens. Additionally, there may be dramatic changes of scale, color, and tonality to maintain interest.

Repetition is sometimes found to be a necessary device for reinforcing visual impact. The image might, for example, be printed as a coarse-screen background image in gray and overprinted with the same image reduced, and printed in a darker tone using a fine screen.

A ghosted halftone is usually used as either a background or in cases where one part of an image requires more prominence than the rest. It is achieved technically by masking out during exposure so that the halftone dots are reduced in strength. Similarly, silhouettes or dropout halftones are used when the background detail needs to be eliminated.

Vignettes are often used for portraiture or period

Right A ghosted image. The lettering has been distorted to follow the contours of the body shape.

Left The spiraling repetition on this CD pack lends an almost three-dimensional quality to the design.

Below right The coarse-weaved texture of the screen, together with the optically jarring background, combine to produce a design which is anything but static!

will within the format of the console screen. Each image is scanned separately prior to collaging. This allows the operator to adjust the size of each image in proportion to the other elements used. Much depends on the skill of the operator and the degree to which he or she is able to interpret the ideas presented by the designer. Sci-tex often mixes hand-drawn and photo-based imagery. It can also be used to create the illusion of three dimensions. The creative implications of such technology are vast.

settings, recalling, perhaps, early photography or 19th-century engravings. The soft edges of the vignette are usually created by airbrushing the edges of the image so that it gradually fades into the white of the paper. The printer can do this for you, but it is always safer to supply the original vignette as you want it.

The once humble office photocopier has now become an exciting, versatile, and refined piece of equipment. The fact that the designer can easily gain access to a copier means that he or she can experiment with distortions, color changes, and different exposures.

Design will for the foreseeable future combine a mix of conventional and new technology. Increasingly, however, electronic systems such as Sci-tex will replace many of the craft-based techniques previously described. The Sci-tex computer enables the designer to produce a collage of images from different sources. Four or five transparencies can be fed into the system and disposed at

Postscript

Halftone effects are only one part of a process – a means to an end. All reproduction techniques which involve high labor costs or the use of expensive machinery will inevitably be expensive. The commercial viability of any job must always be assessed with this in mind. Having said that, what matters is to be able to use these techniques to communicate an idea. The pioneer American designer Paul Rand makes it clear that, *"design which is generated by intuition or by computer, by invention or by a system of co-ordinates – is not good design if it does not co-operate as an instrument in the service of communication."*

Professional applications

Above The original photographic image was scanned into a Barco Creator System (comparable to an Adobe System). Wires used to suspend the lettering were removed electronically, and shadows and reflections accentuated to create a three-dimensional illusion. The warm vignette effect was added by hand.

Right A good example of a solarized image that employs primary colors in a discordant way, which is entirely suited to the subject.

Left and above right These photographs have been vertically and horizontally distorted to emphasize the off-beat opinions of the magazine article which these images were used to illustrate.

Left A reproduction of a two-color duotone produced by using only the cyan and yellow films from a four-color set. In this instance the four color film has been printed in a brown, and the yellow film in a blue. The two special colors used can be seen in the printer's color bar beneath the image.

Above A re-screened photograph of a jazz musician is collaged with ephemeral graphic fragments and overprinted with transparent yellow.

Below On this contemporary dance program, the vertical distortion of the image was achieved using mechanical manipulation.

Right and below right These images have been created with a Paintbox system – grids, pixellation, negative, positive distortion, and solarization can all be readily applied. Special colors have been used and printed in both matte and gloss inks.

dazzling DANGEROUS dance

PHOENIX DANCE COMPANY

8 – 12 OCTOBER

5 – 9 NOVEMBER

SABURO TESHIGAWARA'S COMPANY KARAS DAH-DAH-SKO DAH-DAH

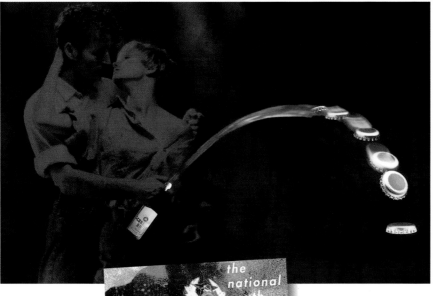

Above An advertisement which combines a scanned black and white photograph with a manipulated image of a bottle, gushing beer and cap to produce a dynamic result, which has obvious sexual connotations.

Right Two closely related colors are used for this image, which employs both a mezzotint screen and partial manipulation by chemical reaction during processing.

Top right A computer-generated collage cover combines fragments of torn halftones of facial features with complementary primary colors and graffiti-like distorted letterforms.

Above This image combines several special halftone effects created using a Paintbox system. On the left, pixellation merges into pixels containing fragments of the halftone image, which in turn merge into the full strength four-color halftone. On the right, the halftone merges into a second halftone image.

Left An effective use of a mezzotint screen to produce a soft, textured image of a face, which contrasts with sharply defined stencil and typewriter letterforms.

Below A transparency reproduced in two ways: the border is a mezzotint screened at a percentage, while the detail in the panel is reproduced normally at full strength. This is one way of making the most of one image if the budget is tight.

Right A composite image produced on a graphic Paintbox. The model's head was photographed in three different positions — bowed, straight-on and leaning back. The images were then merged together with a shot of the inside of a lion's mouth to produce a billboard.

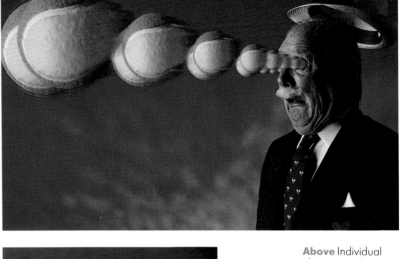

Above A photograph of a speedboat and water-skier was taken in a cornfield. A separate shot of the sky was created and blended in on a Barco Creator System (comparable to an Adobe System). There was additionally some reshaping of the wave-like corn.

Right An effective use of two printings using reversed-out type and a halftone image of a chair printed out-of-register in each color to lend a sense of movement to an otherwise static image.

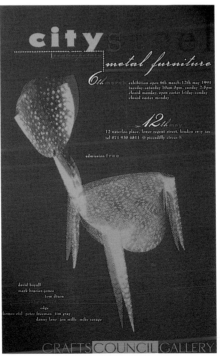

Above Individual elements such as the tennis ball, hat, and background were photographed separately in the studio before being merged and manipulated with the main figure on a Barco Creator System (comparable to an Adobe System).

This section deals with the creative use of halftones when printed in black and white and with a second flat color or special fifth color. Color choices are personal and therefore hugely variable. The three special colors used here represent examples of different tones — light, medium, and dark. The choice of tone will affect the result tremendously.

Printing work in two colors should never be regarded as restrictive. The imaginative use of tints and overprinting can bring life and vitality into a job.

WORKING WITH TWO COLOR

Using this section

To make the most of what can be achieved using black and white halftones, *Halftone Effects* gives you a vast reference library of permutations, specially created by printing black and white on its own and in conjunction with a second color.

The choice of a second color is subjective, but you must always consider how the tone of that color will affect the printed result. To help you, this section uses colors of three different tones – light, medium, and dark. These are three individual flat colors, or fifth colors, which are not created using the four-color process. The choice of color will affect the look of a job tremendously – you must remember that.

When specifying a second color to a printer you must either quote a number from one of the special brand name ink systems, such as PANTONE, or give the printer a color swatch to match the color. When marking up artwork for the printer, always ensure that your instructions are clear and unambiguous. If in doubt, check verbally with your printer that he or she has understood what you want.

Each technique used here is designed to stimulate the design process and to take away some of the risk involved when using these effects commercially. Every printed example of a particular technique is clearly labeled. There are, of course, endless possibilities, and those used here are only a starting point – a source of information and inspiration.

Right The three special colours used in this section. Using a 100 percent tint of the light tone is very different to a 100 percent tint of the dark tone. This section will help you to make decisions about how to use a fifth color.

LIGHT-TONED COLOR • FADING FROM 100% TO 0%

MEDIUM-TONED COLOR • FADING FROM 100% TO 0%

DARK-TONED COLOR • FADING FROM 100% TO 0%

Each technique is explained precisely in the title

The step and repeat image of the eye reinforces the technique employed – at a glance

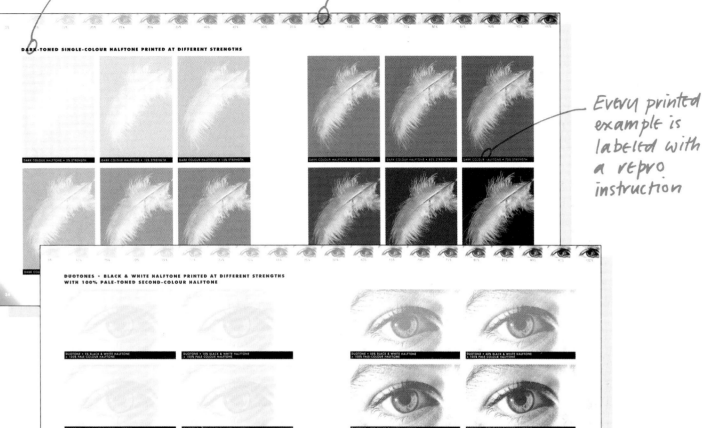

Every printed example is labelled with a repro instruction

DARK-TONED SINGLE-COLOUR HALFTONE PRINTED AT DIFFERENT STRENGTHS

DARK COLOUR HALFTONE + 5% STRENGTH
DARK COLOUR HALFTONE + 10% STRENGTH
DARK COLOUR HALFTONE + 15% STRENGTH
DARK COLOUR HALFTONE + 30% STRENGTH
DARK COLOUR HALFTONE + 60% STRENGTH
DARK COLOUR HALFTONE + 70% STRENGTH

DUOTONES · BLACK & WHITE HALFTONE PRINTED AT DIFFERENT STRENGTHS
WITH 100% PALE-TONED SECOND-COLOUR HALFTONE

DUOTONE + 5% BLACK & WHITE HALFTONE + 100% PALE-COLOUR HALFTONE
DUOTONE + 10% BLACK & WHITE HALFTONE + 100% PALE-COLOUR HALFTONE
DUOTONE + 50% BLACK & WHITE HALFTONE + 100% PALE-COLOUR HALFTONE
DUOTONE + 60% BLACK & WHITE HALFTONE + 100% PALE-COLOUR HALFTONE

DUOTONE + 15% BLACK & WHITE HALFTONE + 100% PALE-COLOUR HALFTONE
DUOTONE + 20% BLACK & WHITE HALFTONE + 100% PALE-COLOUR HALFTONE
DUOTONE + 70% BLACK & WHITE HALFTONE + 100% PALE-COLOUR HALFTONE
DUOTONE + 80% BLACK & WHITE HALFTONE + 100% PALE-COLOUR HALFTONE

DUOTONE + 30% BLACK & WHITE HALFTONE + 100% PALE-COLOUR HALFTONE
DUOTONE + 40% BLACK & WHITE HALFTONE + 100% PALE-COLOUR HALFTONE
DUOTONE + 90% BLACK & WHITE HALFTONE + 100% PALE-COLOUR HALFTONE
DUOTONE + 100% BLACK & WHITE HALFTONE + 100% PALE-COLOUR HALFTONE

the original black and white image used incorporates a wide range of tones and contrast. Check the quality of your own original

Many of the techniques shown have never been published before

Visual charts show the results of effects applied progressively

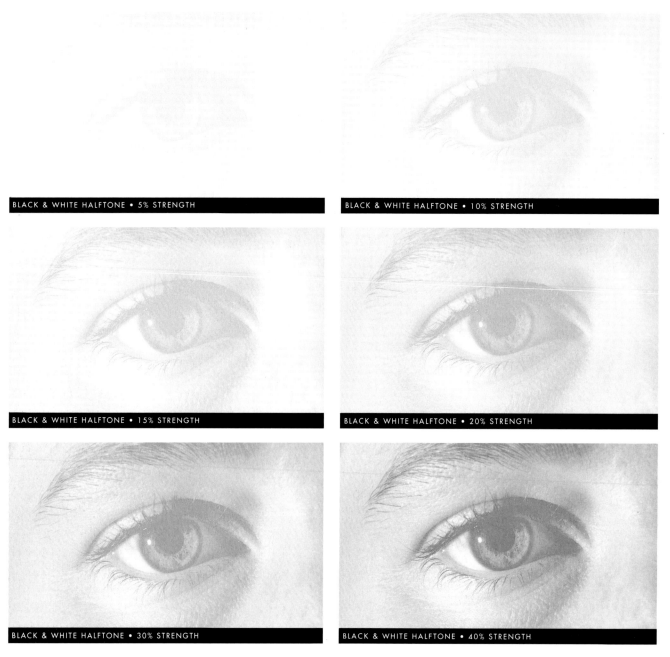

BLACK & WHITE HALFTONE SCANNED AT DIFFERENT STRENGTHS

BLACK & WHITE HALFTONE • 5% STRENGTH

BLACK & WHITE HALFTONE • 10% STRENGTH

BLACK & WHITE HALFTONE • 15% STRENGTH

BLACK & WHITE HALFTONE • 20% STRENGTH

BLACK & WHITE HALFTONE • 30% STRENGTH

BLACK & WHITE HALFTONE • 40% STRENGTH

BLACK & WHITE HALFTONE • 50% STRENGTH

BLACK & WHITE HALFTONE • 60% STRENGTH

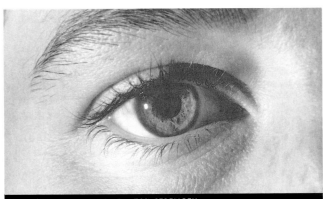
BLACK & WHITE HALFTONE • 70% STRENGTH

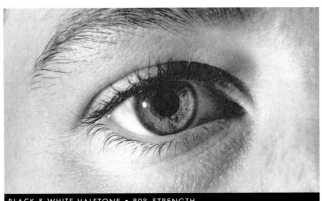
BLACK & WHITE HALFTONE • 80% STRENGTH

BLACK & WHITE HALFTONE • 90% STRENGTH

BLACK & WHITE HALFTONE • 100% STRENGTH

PALE-TONED SINGLE-COLOR HALFTONE PRINTED AT DIFFERENT STRENGTHS

PALE COLOR HALFTONE • 5% STRENGTH

PALE COLOR HALFTONE • 10% STRENGTH

PALE COLOR HALFTONE • 15% STRENGTH

PALE COLOR HALFTONE • 20% STRENGTH

PALE COLOR HALFTONE • 30% STRENGTH

PALE COLOR HALFTONE • 40% STRENGTH

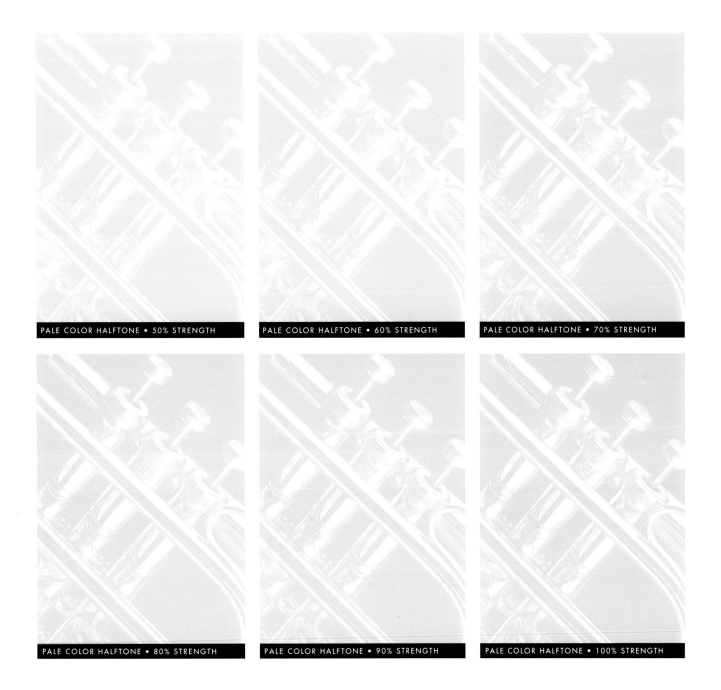

PALE COLOR HALFTONE • 50% STRENGTH

PALE COLOR HALFTONE • 60% STRENGTH

PALE COLOR HALFTONE • 70% STRENGTH

PALE COLOR HALFTONE • 80% STRENGTH

PALE COLOR HALFTONE • 90% STRENGTH

PALE COLOR HALFTONE • 100% STRENGTH

MEDIUM-TONED SINGLE-COLOR HALFTONE PRINTED AT DIFFERENT STRENGTHS

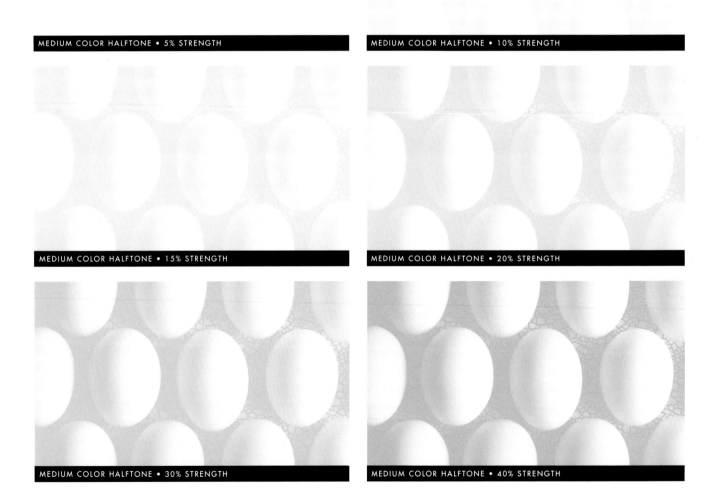

MEDIUM COLOR HALFTONE • 5% STRENGTH

MEDIUM COLOR HALFTONE • 10% STRENGTH

MEDIUM COLOR HALFTONE • 15% STRENGTH

MEDIUM COLOR HALFTONE • 20% STRENGTH

MEDIUM COLOR HALFTONE • 30% STRENGTH

MEDIUM COLOR HALFTONE • 40% STRENGTH

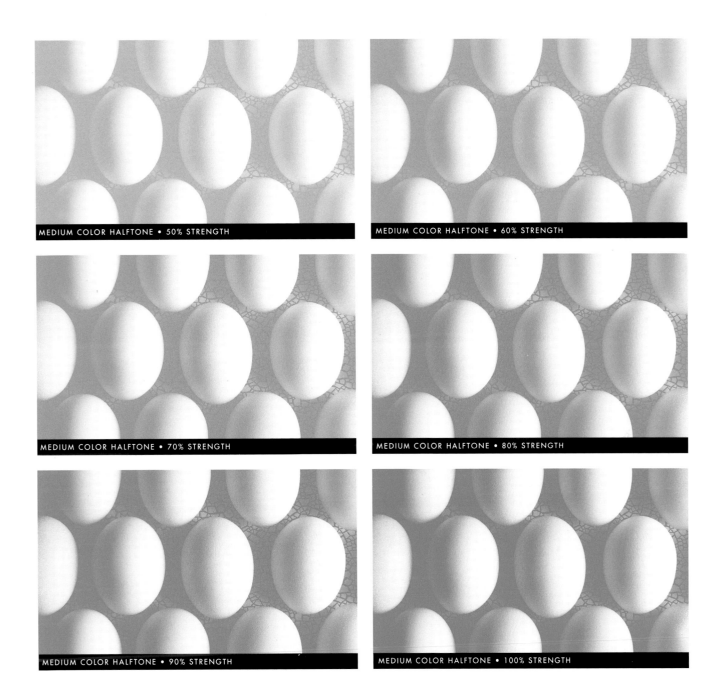

MEDIUM COLOR HALFTONE • 50% STRENGTH

MEDIUM COLOR HALFTONE • 60% STRENGTH

MEDIUM COLOR HALFTONE • 70% STRENGTH

MEDIUM COLOR HALFTONE • 80% STRENGTH

MEDIUM COLOR HALFTONE • 90% STRENGTH

MEDIUM COLOR HALFTONE • 100% STRENGTH

DARK-TONED SINGLE-COLOR HALFTONE PRINTED AT DIFFERENT STRENGTHS

DARK COLOR HALFTONE • 5% STRENGTH

DARK COLOR HALFTONE • 10% STRENGTH

DARK COLOR HALFTONE • 15% STRENGTH

DARK COLOR HALFTONE • 20% STRENGTH

DARK COLOR HALFTONE • 30% STRENGTH

DARK COLOR HALFTONE • 40% STRENGTH

DARK COLOR HALFTONE • 50% STRENGTH

DARK COLOR HALFTONE • 60% STRENGTH

DARK COLOR HALFTONE • 70% STRENGTH

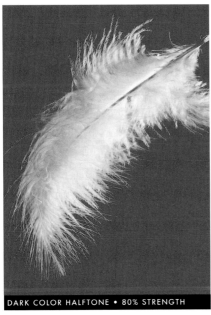

DARK COLOR HALFTONE • 80% STRENGTH

DARK COLOR HALFTONE • 90% STRENGTH

DARK COLOR HALFTONE • 100% STRENGTH

BLACK & WHITE HALFTONE PRINTED AT DIFFERENT STRENGTHS OVER SOLID PALE-TONED SECOND COLOR

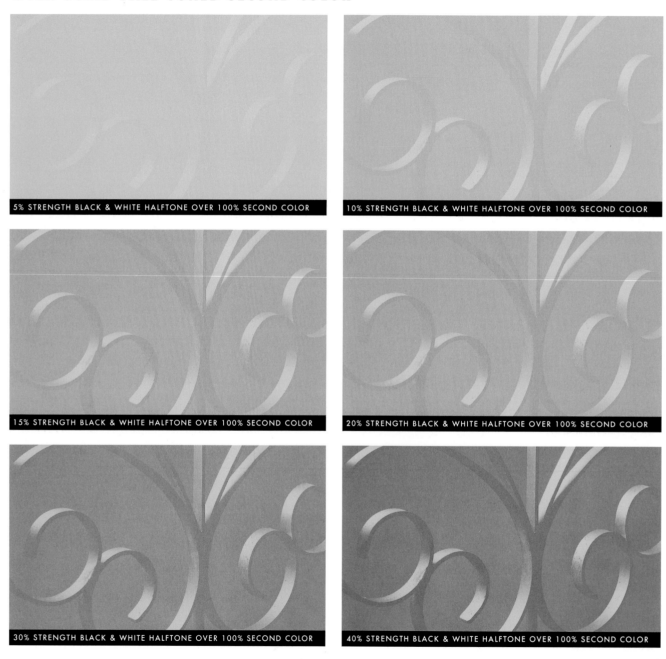

5% STRENGTH BLACK & WHITE HALFTONE OVER 100% SECOND COLOR

10% STRENGTH BLACK & WHITE HALFTONE OVER 100% SECOND COLOR

15% STRENGTH BLACK & WHITE HALFTONE OVER 100% SECOND COLOR

20% STRENGTH BLACK & WHITE HALFTONE OVER 100% SECOND COLOR

30% STRENGTH BLACK & WHITE HALFTONE OVER 100% SECOND COLOR

40% STRENGTH BLACK & WHITE HALFTONE OVER 100% SECOND COLOR

50% STRENGTH BLACK & WHITE HALFTONE OVER 100% SECOND COLOR

60% STRENGTH BLACK & WHITE HALFTONE OVER 100% SECOND COLOR

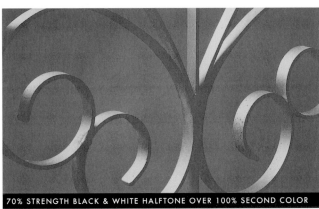

70% STRENGTH BLACK & WHITE HALFTONE OVER 100% SECOND COLOR

80% STRENGTH BLACK & WHITE HALFTONE OVER 100% SECOND COLOR

90% STRENGTH BLACK & WHITE HALFTONE OVER 100% SECOND COLOR

100% STRENGTH BLACK & WHITE HALFTONE OVER 100% SECOND COLOR

BLACK & WHITE HALFTONE PRINTED AT DIFFERENT STRENGTHS OVER SOLID MEDIUM-TONED SECOND COLOR

5% STRENGTH BLACK & WHITE HALFTONE
OVER 100% SECOND COLOR

10% STRENGTH BLACK & WHITE HALFTONE
OVER 100% SECOND COLOR

15% STRENGTH BLACK & WHITE HALFTONE
OVER 100% SECOND COLOR

20% STRENGTH BLACK & WHITE HALFTONE
OVER 100% SECOND COLOR

30% STRENGTH BLACK & WHITE HALFTONE
OVER 100% SECOND COLOR

40% STRENGTH BLACK & WHITE HALFTONE
OVER 100% SECOND COLOR

50% STRENGTH BLACK & WHITE HALFTONE
OVER 100% SECOND COLOR

60% STRENGTH BLACK & WHITE HALFTONE
OVER 100% SECOND COLOR

70% STRENGTH BLACK & WHITE HALFTONE
OVER 100% SECOND COLOR

80% STRENGTH BLACK & WHITE HALFTONE
OVER 100% SECOND COLOR

90% STRENGTH BLACK & WHITE HALFTONE
OVER 100% SECOND COLOR

100% STRENGTH BLACK & WHITE HALFTONE
OVER 100% SECOND COLOR

BLACK & WHITE HALFTONE PRINTED AT DIFFERENT STRENGTHS
OVER SOLID DARK-TONED SECOND COLOR

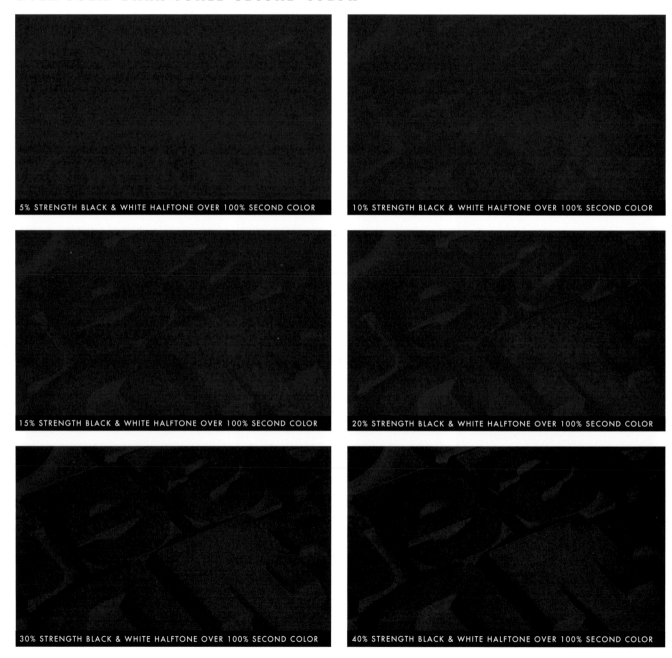

5% STRENGTH BLACK & WHITE HALFTONE OVER 100% SECOND COLOR

10% STRENGTH BLACK & WHITE HALFTONE OVER 100% SECOND COLOR

15% STRENGTH BLACK & WHITE HALFTONE OVER 100% SECOND COLOR

20% STRENGTH BLACK & WHITE HALFTONE OVER 100% SECOND COLOR

30% STRENGTH BLACK & WHITE HALFTONE OVER 100% SECOND COLOR

40% STRENGTH BLACK & WHITE HALFTONE OVER 100% SECOND COLOR

50% STRENGTH BLACK & WHITE HALFTONE OVER 100% SECOND COLOR

60% STRENGTH BLACK & WHITE HALFTONE OVER 100% SECOND COLOR

70% STRENGTH BLACK & WHITE HALFTONE OVER 100% SECOND COLOR

80% STRENGTH BLACK & WHITE HALFTONE OVER 100% SECOND COLOR

90% STRENGTH BLACK & WHITE HALFTONE OVER 100% SECOND COLOR

100% STRENGTH BLACK & WHITE HALFTONE OVER 100% SECOND COLOR

BLACK & WHITE HALFTONE PRINTED OVER
PALE-TONED SECOND-COLOR FLAT TINTS OF DIFFERENT STRENGTHS

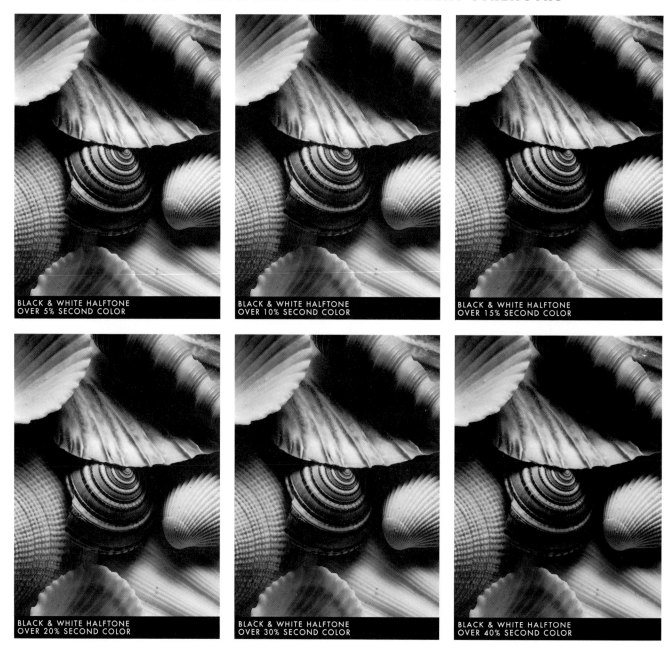

BLACK & WHITE HALFTONE
OVER 5% SECOND COLOR

BLACK & WHITE HALFTONE
OVER 10% SECOND COLOR

BLACK & WHITE HALFTONE
OVER 15% SECOND COLOR

BLACK & WHITE HALFTONE
OVER 20% SECOND COLOR

BLACK & WHITE HALFTONE
OVER 30% SECOND COLOR

BLACK & WHITE HALFTONE
OVER 40% SECOND COLOR

BLACK & WHITE HALFTONE
OVER 50% SECOND COLOR

BLACK & WHITE HALFTONE
OVER 60% SECOND COLOR

BLACK & WHITE HALFTONE
OVER 70% SECOND COLOR

BLACK & WHITE HALFTONE
OVER 80% SECOND COLOR

BLACK & WHITE HALFTONE
OVER 90% SECOND COLOR

BLACK & WHITE HALFTONE
OVER 100% SECOND COLOR

BLACK & WHITE HALFTONE PRINTED OVER
MEDIUM-TONED SECOND-COLOR FLAT TINTS OF DIFFERENT STRENGTHS

BLACK & WHITE HALFTONE OVER 5% STRENGTH SECOND COLOR

BLACK & WHITE HALFTONE OVER 10% STRENGTH SECOND COLOR

BLACK & WHITE HALFTONE OVER 15% STRENGTH SECOND COLOR

BLACK & WHITE HALFTONE OVER 20% STRENGTH SECOND COLOR

BLACK & WHITE HALFTONE OVER 30% STRENGTH SECOND COLOR

BLACK & WHITE HALFTONE OVER 40% STRENGTH SECOND COLOR

BLACK & WHITE HALFTONE OVER 50% STRENGTH SECOND COLOR

BLACK & WHITE HALFTONE OVER 60% STRENGTH SECOND COLOR

BLACK & WHITE HALFTONE OVER 70% STRENGTH SECOND COLOR

BLACK & WHITE HALFTONE OVER 80% STRENGTH SECOND COLOR

BLACK & WHITE HALFTONE OVER 90% STRENGTH SECOND COLOR

BLACK & WHITE HALFTONE OVER 100% STRENGTH SECOND COLOR

BLACK & WHITE HALFTONE PRINTED OVER
DARK-TONED SECOND-COLOR FLAT TINTS OF DIFFERENT STRENGTHS

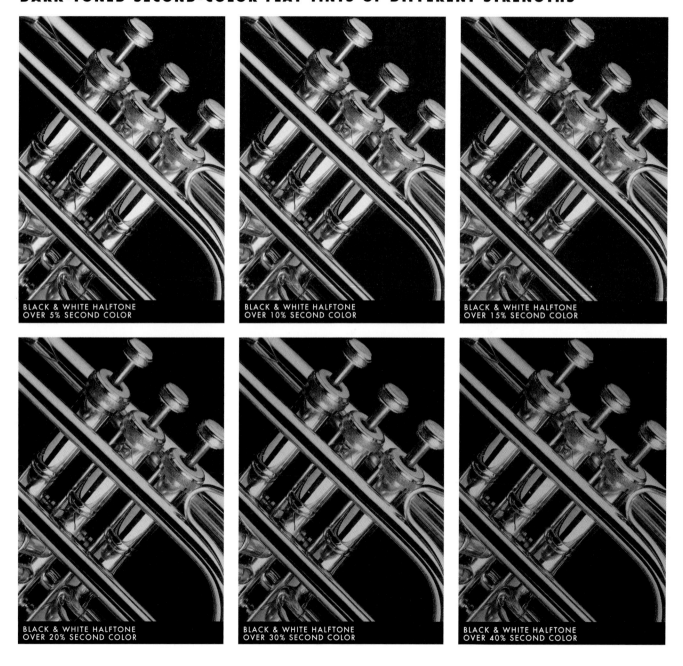

BLACK & WHITE HALFTONE
OVER 5% SECOND COLOR

BLACK & WHITE HALFTONE
OVER 10% SECOND COLOR

BLACK & WHITE HALFTONE
OVER 15% SECOND COLOR

BLACK & WHITE HALFTONE
OVER 20% SECOND COLOR

BLACK & WHITE HALFTONE
OVER 30% SECOND COLOR

BLACK & WHITE HALFTONE
OVER 40% SECOND COLOR

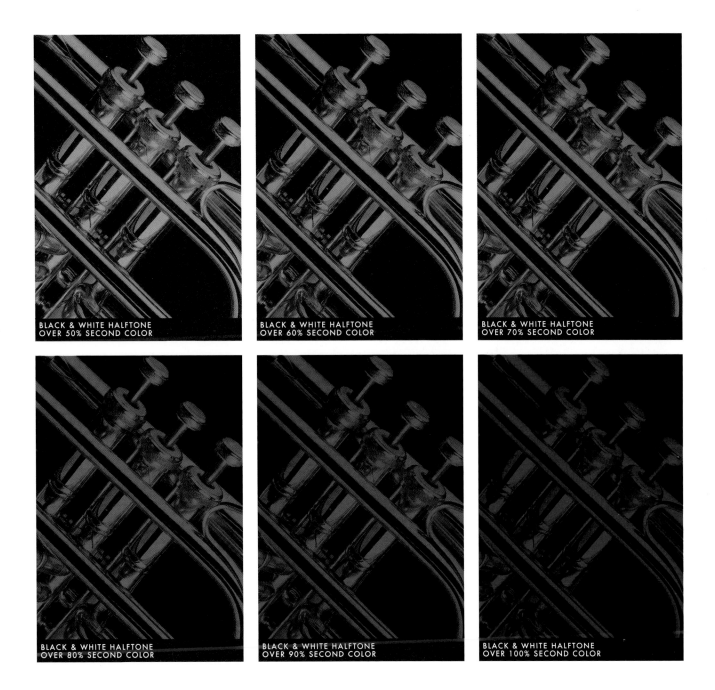

BLACK & WHITE HALFTONE
OVER 50% SECOND COLOR

BLACK & WHITE HALFTONE
OVER 60% SECOND COLOR

BLACK & WHITE HALFTONE
OVER 70% SECOND COLOR

BLACK & WHITE HALFTONE
OVER 80% SECOND COLOR

BLACK & WHITE HALFTONE
OVER 90% SECOND COLOR

BLACK & WHITE HALFTONE
OVER 100% SECOND COLOR

PALE-TONED SECOND-COLOR HALFTONE REVERSED OUT OF/ PRINTED OVER DIFFERENT-STRENGTH BLACK TINTS

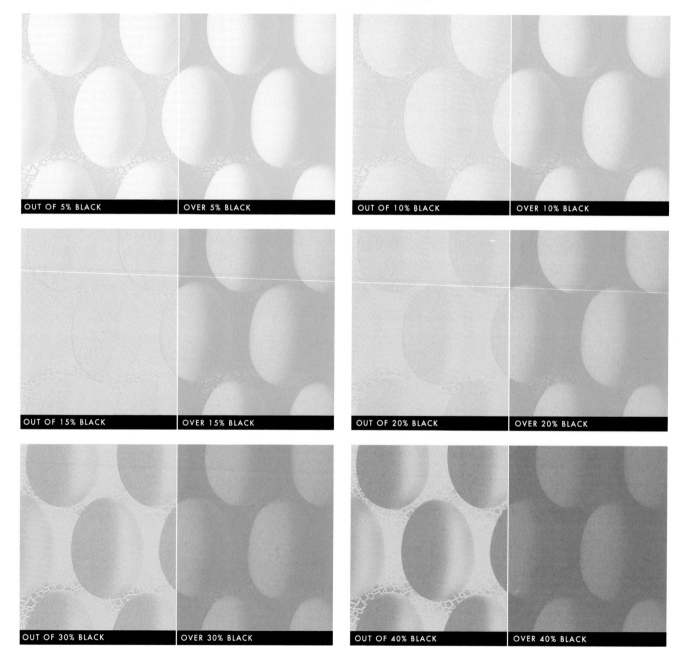

OUT OF 5% BLACK | OVER 5% BLACK

OUT OF 10% BLACK | OVER 10% BLACK

OUT OF 15% BLACK | OVER 15% BLACK

OUT OF 20% BLACK | OVER 20% BLACK

OUT OF 30% BLACK | OVER 30% BLACK

OUT OF 40% BLACK | OVER 40% BLACK

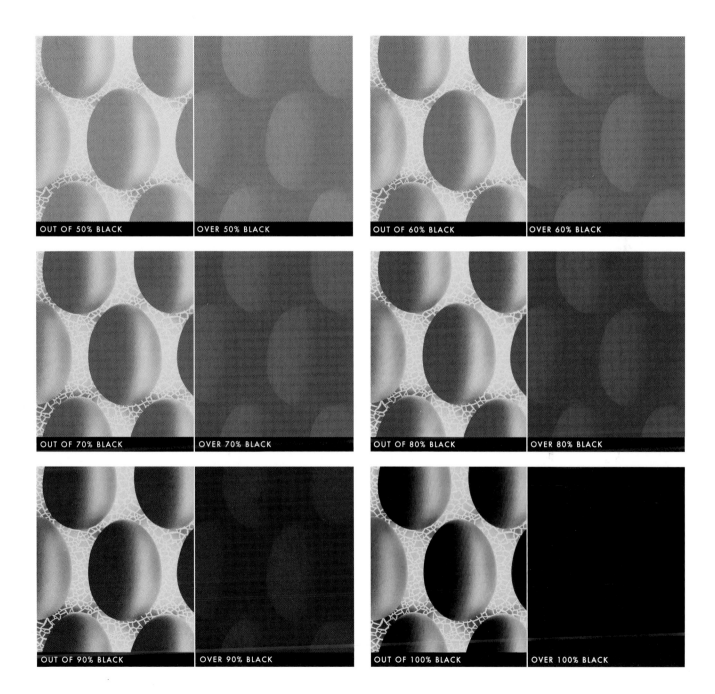

OUT OF 50% BLACK

OVER 50% BLACK

OUT OF 60% BLACK

OVER 60% BLACK

OUT OF 70% BLACK

OVER 70% BLACK

OUT OF 80% BLACK

OVER 80% BLACK

OUT OF 90% BLACK

OVER 90% BLACK

OUT OF 100% BLACK

OVER 100% BLACK

MEDIUM-TONED SECOND-COLOR HALFTONE REVERSED OUT OF/
PRINTED OVER DIFFERENT-STRENGTH BLACK TINTS

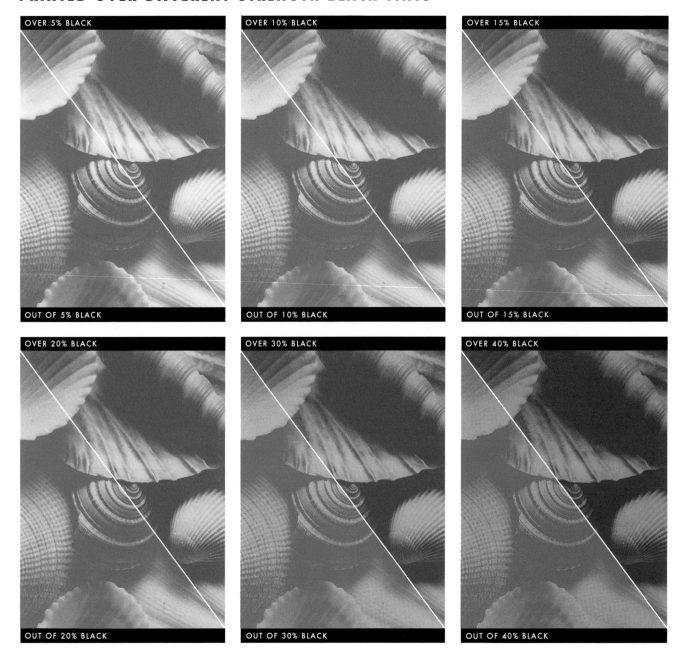

OVER 5% BLACK

OUT OF 5% BLACK

OVER 10% BLACK

OUT OF 10% BLACK

OVER 15% BLACK

OUT OF 15% BLACK

OVER 20% BLACK

OUT OF 20% BLACK

OVER 30% BLACK

OUT OF 30% BLACK

OVER 40% BLACK

OUT OF 40% BLACK

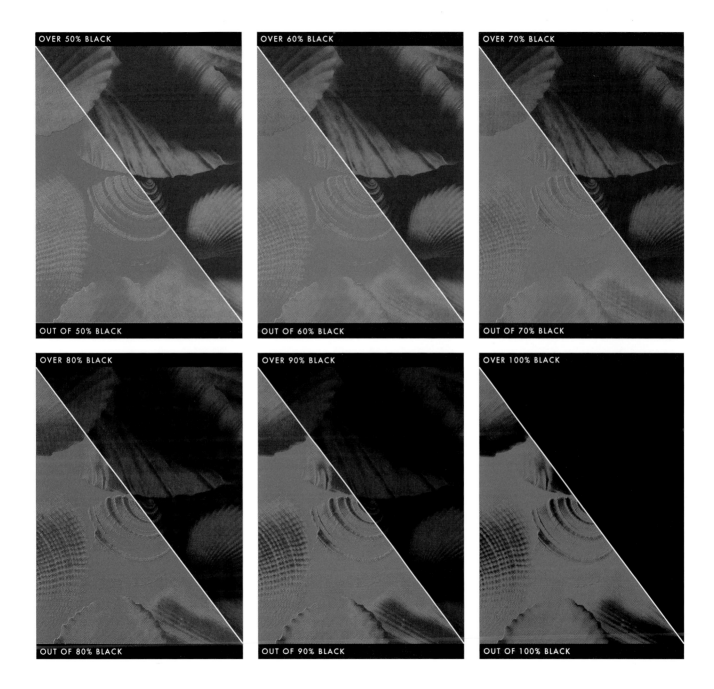

OVER 50% BLACK

OUT OF 50% BLACK

OVER 60% BLACK

OUT OF 60% BLACK

OVER 70% BLACK

OUT OF 70% BLACK

OVER 80% BLACK

OUT OF 80% BLACK

OVER 90% BLACK

OUT OF 90% BLACK

OVER 100% BLACK

OUT OF 100% BLACK

DARK-TONED SECOND-COLOR HALFTONE REVERSED OUT OF/
PRINTED OVER DIFFERENT-STRENGTH BLACK TINTS

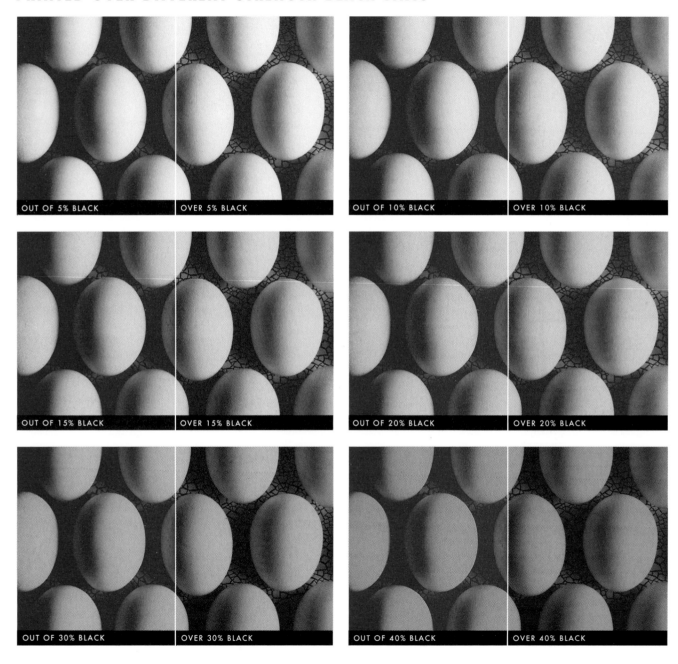

OUT OF 5% BLACK   OVER 5% BLACK   OUT OF 10% BLACK   OVER 10% BLACK

OUT OF 15% BLACK   OVER 15% BLACK   OUT OF 20% BLACK   OVER 20% BLACK

OUT OF 30% BLACK   OVER 30% BLACK   OUT OF 40% BLACK   OVER 40% BLACK

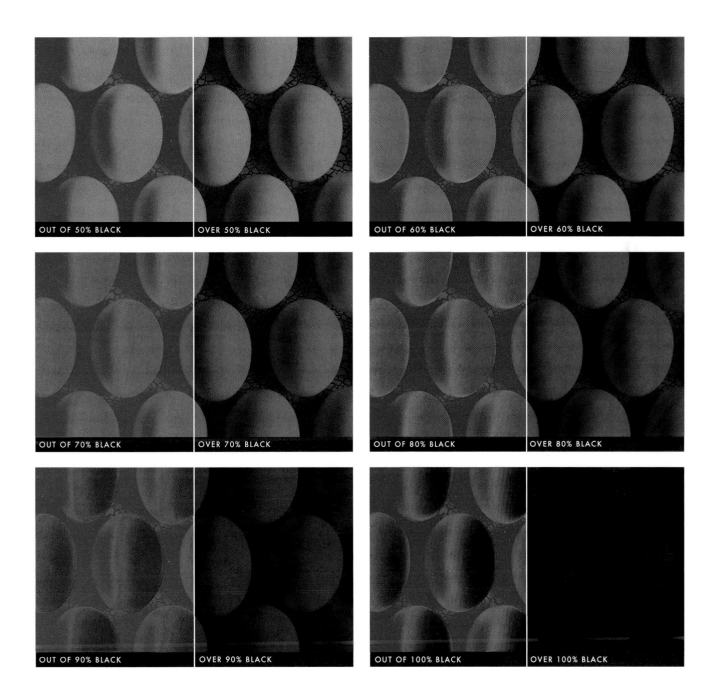

OUT OF 50% BLACK

OVER 50% BLACK

OUT OF 60% BLACK

OVER 60% BLACK

OUT OF 70% BLACK

OVER 70% BLACK

OUT OF 80% BLACK

OVER 80% BLACK

OUT OF 90% BLACK

OVER 90% BLACK

OUT OF 100% BLACK

OVER 100% BLACK

DUOTONE • 5% PALE COLOR HALFTONE
+ 100% BLACK & WHITE HALFTONE

DUOTONE • 10% PALE COLOR HALFTONE
+ 100% BLACK & WHITE HALFTONE

DUOTONE • 15% PALE COLOR HALFTONE
+ 100% BLACK & WHITE HALFTONE

DUOTONE • 20% PALE COLOR HALFTONE
+ 100% BLACK & WHITE HALFTONE

DUOTONE • 30% PALE COLOR HALFTONE
+ 100% BLACK & WHITE HALFTONE

DUOTONE • 40% PALE COLOR HALFTONE
+ 100% BLACK & WHITE HALFTONE

DUOTONE • 50% PALE COLOR HALFTONE
+ 100% BLACK & WHITE HALFTONE

DUOTONE • 60% PALE COLOR HALFTONE
+ 100% BLACK & WHITE HALFTONE

DUOTONE • 70% PALE COLOR HALFTONE
+ 100% BLACK & WHITE HALFTONE

DUOTONE • 80% PALE COLOR HALFTONE
+ 100% BLACK & WHITE HALFTONE

DUOTONE • 90% PALE COLOR HALFTONE
+ 100% BLACK & WHITE HALFTONE

DUOTONE • 100% PALE COLOR HALFTONE
+ 100% BLACK & WHITE HALFTONE

DUOTONES • MEDIUM-TONED SECOND-COLOR HALFTONE
PRINTED AT DIFFERENT STRENGTHS WITH 100% BLACK & WHITE HALFTONE

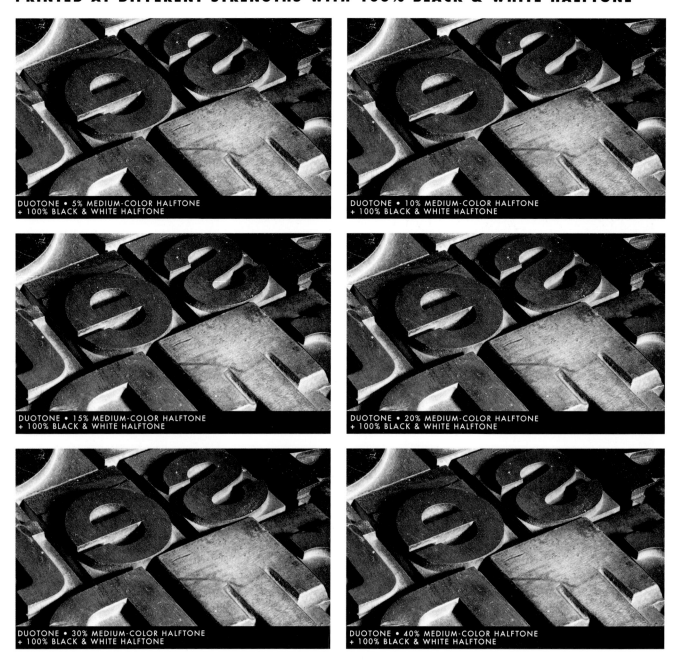

DUOTONE • 5% MEDIUM-COLOR HALFTONE
+ 100% BLACK & WHITE HALFTONE

DUOTONE • 10% MEDIUM-COLOR HALFTONE
+ 100% BLACK & WHITE HALFTONE

DUOTONE • 15% MEDIUM-COLOR HALFTONE
+ 100% BLACK & WHITE HALFTONE

DUOTONE • 20% MEDIUM-COLOR HALFTONE
+ 100% BLACK & WHITE HALFTONE

DUOTONE • 30% MEDIUM-COLOR HALFTONE
+ 100% BLACK & WHITE HALFTONE

DUOTONE • 40% MEDIUM-COLOR HALFTONE
+ 100% BLACK & WHITE HALFTONE

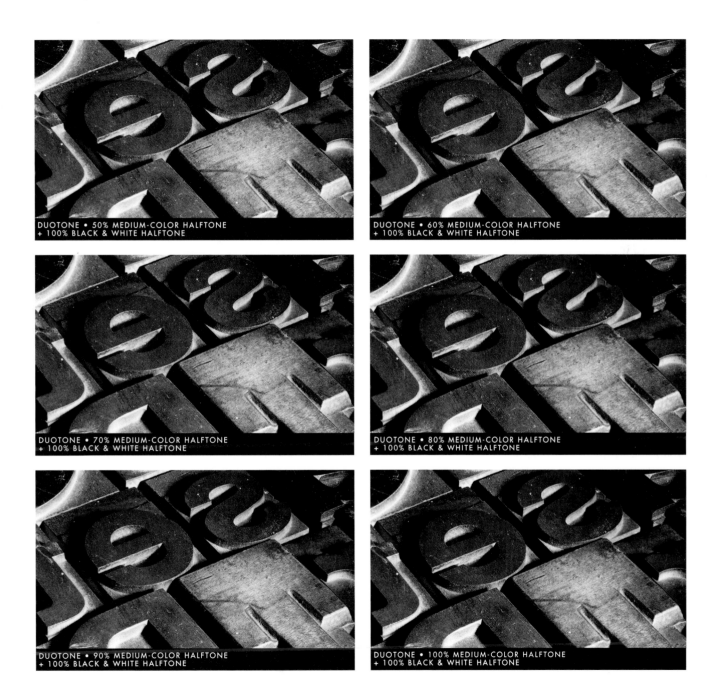

DUOTONE • 50% MEDIUM-COLOR HALFTONE
+ 100% BLACK & WHITE HALFTONE

DUOTONE • 60% MEDIUM-COLOR HALFTONE
+ 100% BLACK & WHITE HALFTONE

DUOTONE • 70% MEDIUM-COLOR HALFTONE
+ 100% BLACK & WHITE HALFTONE

DUOTONE • 80% MEDIUM-COLOR HALFTONE
+ 100% BLACK & WHITE HALFTONE

DUOTONE • 90% MEDIUM-COLOR HALFTONE
+ 100% BLACK & WHITE HALFTONE

DUOTONE • 100% MEDIUM-COLOR HALFTONE
+ 100% BLACK & WHITE HALFTONE

DUOTONES • DARK-TONED SECOND-COLOR HALFTONE
PRINTED AT DIFFERENT STRENGTHS WITH 100% BLACK & WHITE HALFTONE

DUOTONE • 5% DARK-COLOR HALFTONE
+ 100% BLACK & WHITE HALFTONE

DUOTONE • 10% DARK-COLOR HALFTONE
+ 100% BLACK & WHITE HALFTONE

DUOTONE •15% DARK-COLOR HALFTONE
+ 100% BLACK & WHITE HALFTONE

DUOTONE • 20% DARK-COLOR HALFTONE
+ 100% BLACK & WHITE HALFTONE

DUOTONE • 30% DARK-COLOR HALFTONE
+ 100% BLACK & WHITE HALFTONE

DUOTONE • 40% DARK-COLOR HALFTONE
+ 100% BLACK & WHITE HALFTONE

DUOTONE • 50% DARK-COLOR HALFTONE
+ 100% BLACK & WHITE HALFTONE

DUOTONE • 60% DARK-COLOR HALFTONE
+ 100% BLACK & WHITE HALFTONE

DUOTONE • 70% DARK-COLOR HALFTONE
+ 100% BLACK & WHITE HALFTONE

DUOTONE • 80% DARK-COLOR HALFTONE
+ 100% BLACK & WHITE HALFTONE

DUOTONE • 90% DARK-COLOR HALFTONE
+ 100% BLACK & WHITE HALFTONE

DUOTONE • 100% DARK-COLOR HALFTONE
+ 100% BLACK & WHITE HALFTONE

DUOTONES • BLACK & WHITE HALFTONE PRINTED AT DIFFERENT STRENGTHS WITH 100% PALE-TONED SECOND-COLOR HALFTONE

DUOTONE • 5% BLACK & WHITE HALFTONE
+ 100% PALE-COLOR HALFTONE

DUOTONE • 10% BLACK & WHITE HALFTONE
+ 100% PALE-COLOR HALFTONE

DUOTONE • 15% BLACK & WHITE HALFTONE
+ 100% PALE-COLOR HALFTONE

DUOTONE • 20% BLACK & WHITE HALFTONE
+ 100% PALE-COLOR HALFTONE

DUOTONE • 30% BLACK & WHITE HALFTONE
+ 100% PALE-COLOR HALFTONE

DUOTONE • 40% BLACK & WHITE HALFTONE
+ 100% PALE-COLOR HALFTONE

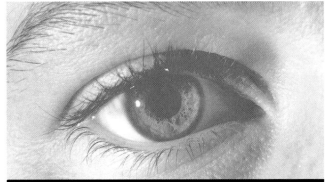

DUOTONE • 50% BLACK & WHITE HALFTONE
+ 100% PALE-COLOR HALFTONE

DUOTONE • 60% BLACK & WHITE HALFTONE
+ 100% PALE-COLOR HALFTONE

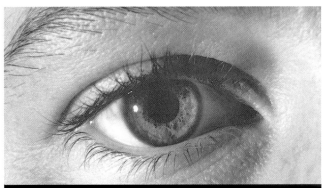

DUOTONE • 70% BLACK & WHITE HALFTONE
+ 100% PALE-COLOR HALFTONE

DUOTONE • 80% BLACK & WHITE HALFTONE
+ 100% PALE-COLOR HALFTONE

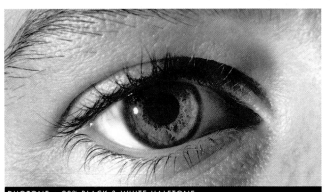

DUOTONE • 90% BLACK & WHITE HALFTONE
+ 100% PALE-COLOR HALFTONE

DUOTONE • 100% BLACK & WHITE HALFTONE
+ 100% PALE-COLOR HALFTONE

DUOTONES • BLACK & WHITE HALFTONE PRINTED AT DIFFERENT STRENGTHS WITH 100% MEDIUM-TONED SECOND-COLOR HALFTONE

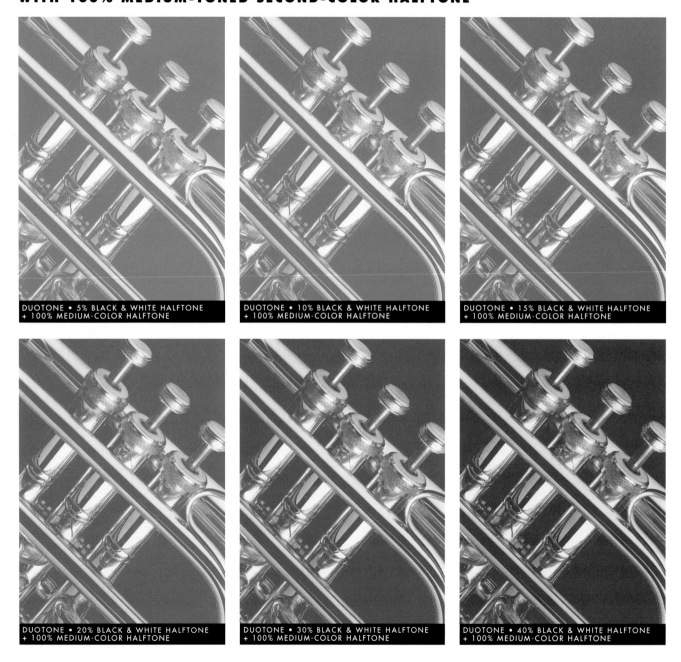

DUOTONE • 5% BLACK & WHITE HALFTONE + 100% MEDIUM-COLOR HALFTONE

DUOTONE • 10% BLACK & WHITE HALFTONE + 100% MEDIUM-COLOR HALFTONE

DUOTONE • 15% BLACK & WHITE HALFTONE + 100% MEDIUM-COLOR HALFTONE

DUOTONE • 20% BLACK & WHITE HALFTONE + 100% MEDIUM-COLOR HALFTONE

DUOTONE • 30% BLACK & WHITE HALFTONE + 100% MEDIUM-COLOR HALFTONE

DUOTONE • 40% BLACK & WHITE HALFTONE + 100% MEDIUM-COLOR HALFTONE

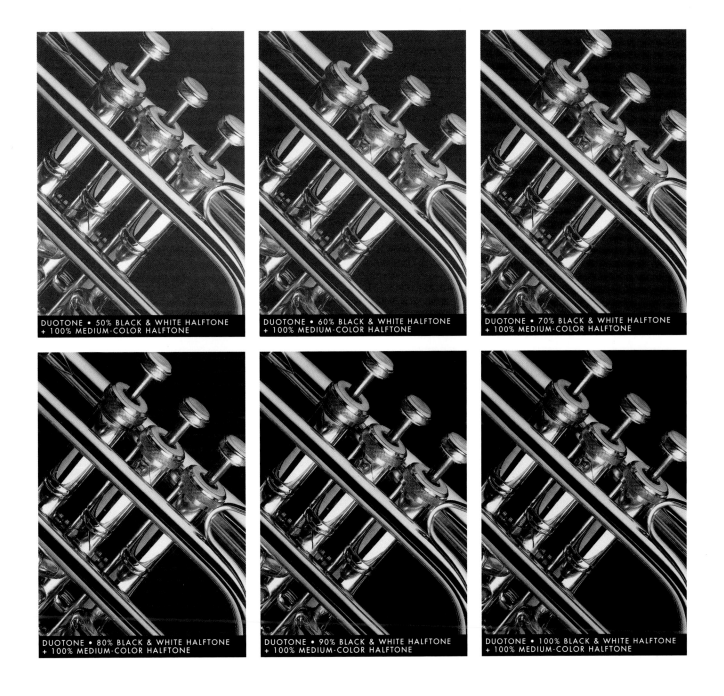

DUOTONE • 50% BLACK & WHITE HALFTONE
+ 100% MEDIUM-COLOR HALFTONE

DUOTONE • 60% BLACK & WHITE HALFTONE
+ 100% MEDIUM-COLOR HALFTONE

DUOTONE • 70% BLACK & WHITE HALFTONE
+ 100% MEDIUM-COLOR HALFTONE

DUOTONE • 80% BLACK & WHITE HALFTONE
+ 100% MEDIUM-COLOR HALFTONE

DUOTONE • 90% BLACK & WHITE HALFTONE
+ 100% MEDIUM-COLOR HALFTONE

DUOTONE • 100% BLACK & WHITE HALFTONE
+ 100% MEDIUM-COLOR HALFTONE

DUOTONES • BLACK & WHITE HALFTONE PRINTED AT DIFFERENT STRENGTHS WITH 100% DARK-TONED SECOND-COLOR HALFTONE

DUOTONE • 5% BLACK & WHITE HALFTONE
+ 100% DARK-COLOR HALFTONE

DUOTONE • 10% BLACK & WHITE HALFTONE
+ 100% DARK-COLOR HALFTONE

DUOTONE • 15% BLACK & WHITE HALFTONE
+ 100% DARK-COLOR HALFTONE

DUOTONE • 20% BLACK & WHITE HALFTONE
+ 100% DARK-COLOR HALFTONE

DUOTONE • 30% BLACK & WHITE HALFTONE
+ 100% DARK-COLOR HALFTONE

DUOTONE • 40% BLACK & WHITE HALFTONE
+ 100% DARK-COLOR HALFTONE

DUOTONE • 50% BLACK & WHITE HALFTONE
+ 100% DARK-COLOR HALFTONE

DUOTONE • 60% BLACK & WHITE HALFTONE
+ 100% DARK-COLOR HALFTONE

DUOTONE • 70% BLACK & WHITE HALFTONE
+ 100% DARK-COLOR HALFTONE

DUOTONE • 80% BLACK & WHITE HALFTONE
+ 100% DARK-COLOR HALFTONE

DUOTONE • 90% BLACK & WHITE HALFTONE
+ 100% DARK-COLOR HALFTONE

DUOTONE • 100% BLACK & WHITE HALFTONE
+ 100% DARK-COLOR HALFTONE

DUOTONES · LIGHT-TONED HALFTONE PRINTED AT DIFFERENT STRENGTHS WITH 100% MEDIUM-TONED SECOND-COLOR HALFTONE

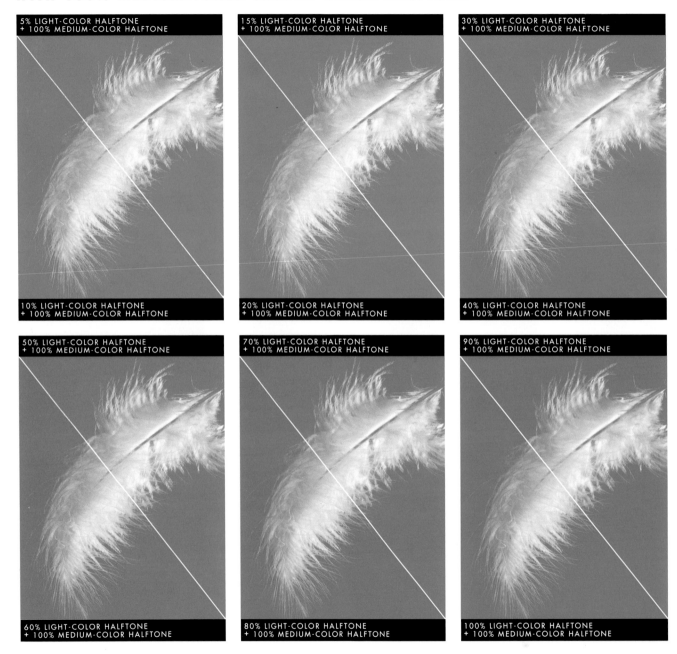

5% LIGHT-COLOR HALFTONE
+ 100% MEDIUM-COLOR HALFTONE

15% LIGHT-COLOR HALFTONE
+ 100% MEDIUM-COLOR HALFTONE

30% LIGHT-COLOR HALFTONE
+ 100% MEDIUM-COLOR HALFTONE

10% LIGHT-COLOR HALFTONE
+ 100% MEDIUM-COLOR HALFTONE

20% LIGHT-COLOR HALFTONE
+ 100% MEDIUM-COLOR HALFTONE

40% LIGHT-COLOR HALFTONE
+ 100% MEDIUM-COLOR HALFTONE

50% LIGHT-COLOR HALFTONE
+ 100% MEDIUM-COLOR HALFTONE

70% LIGHT-COLOR HALFTONE
+ 100% MEDIUM-COLOR HALFTONE

90% LIGHT-COLOR HALFTONE
+ 100% MEDIUM-COLOR HALFTONE

60% LIGHT-COLOR HALFTONE
+ 100% MEDIUM-COLOR HALFTONE

80% LIGHT-COLOR HALFTONE
+ 100% MEDIUM-COLOR HALFTONE

100% LIGHT-COLOR HALFTONE
+ 100% MEDIUM-COLOR HALFTONE

DUOTONES • MEDIUM-TONED HALFTONE PRINTED AT DIFFERENT STRENGTHS WITH 100% LIGHT-TONED SECOND-COLOR HALFTONE

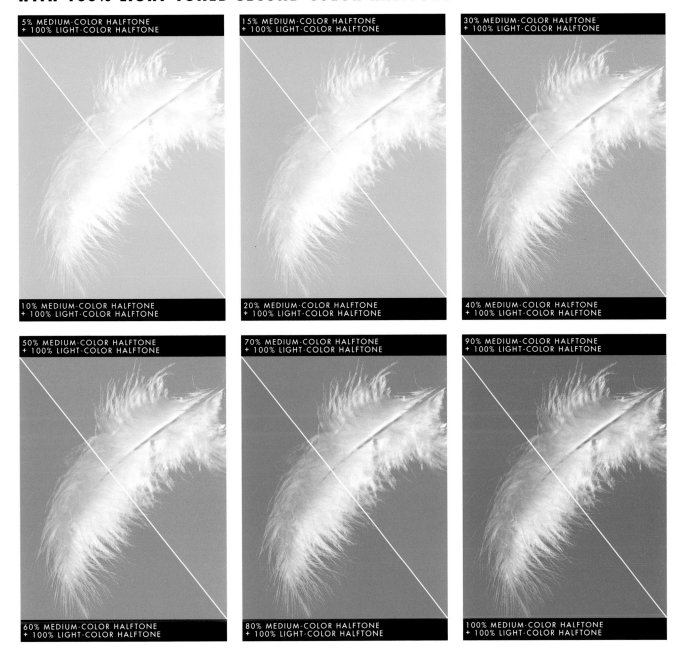

5% MEDIUM-COLOR HALFTONE + 100% LIGHT-COLOR HALFTONE

15% MEDIUM-COLOR HALFTONE + 100% LIGHT-COLOR HALFTONE

30% MEDIUM-COLOR HALFTONE + 100% LIGHT-COLOR HALFTONE

10% MEDIUM-COLOR HALFTONE + 100% LIGHT-COLOR HALFTONE

20% MEDIUM-COLOR HALFTONE + 100% LIGHT-COLOR HALFTONE

40% MEDIUM-COLOR HALFTONE + 100% LIGHT-COLOR HALFTONE

50% MEDIUM-COLOR HALFTONE + 100% LIGHT-COLOR HALFTONE

70% MEDIUM-COLOR HALFTONE + 100% LIGHT-COLOR HALFTONE

90% MEDIUM-COLOR HALFTONE + 100% LIGHT-COLOR HALFTONE

60% MEDIUM-COLOR HALFTONE + 100% LIGHT-COLOR HALFTONE

80% MEDIUM-COLOR HALFTONE + 100% LIGHT-COLOR HALFTONE

100% MEDIUM-COLOR HALFTONE + 100% LIGHT-COLOR HALFTONE

DUOTONES • LIGHT-TONED HALFTONE PRINTED AT DIFFERENT STRENGTHS WITH 100% DARK-TONED SECOND-COLOR HALFTONE

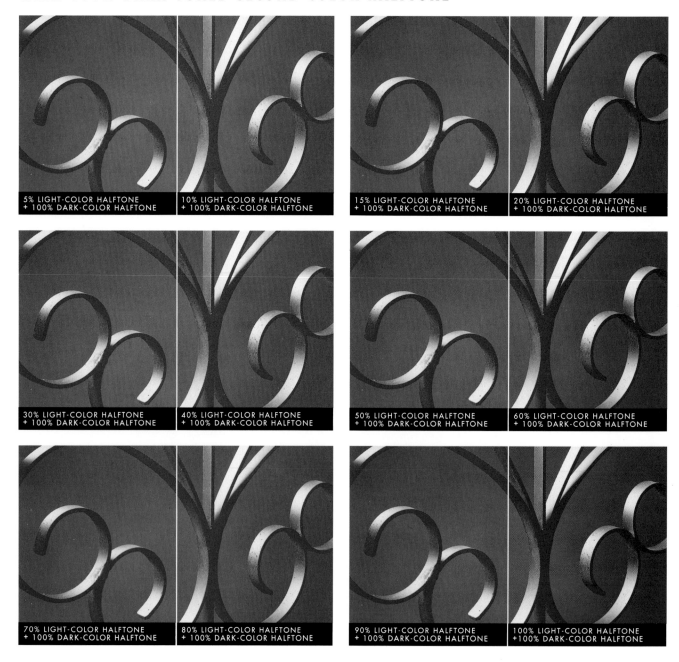

5% LIGHT-COLOR HALFTONE
+ 100% DARK-COLOR HALFTONE

10% LIGHT-COLOR HALFTONE
+ 100% DARK-COLOR HALFTONE

15% LIGHT-COLOR HALFTONE
+ 100% DARK-COLOR HALFTONE

20% LIGHT-COLOR HALFTONE
+ 100% DARK-COLOR HALFTONE

30% LIGHT-COLOR HALFTONE
+ 100% DARK-COLOR HALFTONE

40% LIGHT-COLOR HALFTONE
+ 100% DARK-COLOR HALFTONE

50% LIGHT-COLOR HALFTONE
+ 100% DARK-COLOR HALFTONE

60% LIGHT-COLOR HALFTONE
+ 100% DARK-COLOR HALFTONE

70% LIGHT-COLOR HALFTONE
+ 100% DARK-COLOR HALFTONE

80% LIGHT-COLOR HALFTONE
+ 100% DARK-COLOR HALFTONE

90% LIGHT-COLOR HALFTONE
+ 100% DARK-COLOR HALFTONE

100% LIGHT-COLOR HALFTONE
+ 100% DARK-COLOR HALFTONE

DUOTONES • DARK-TONED HALFTONE PRINTED AT DIFFERENT STRENGTHS WITH 100% LIGHT-TONED SECOND-COLOR HALFTONE

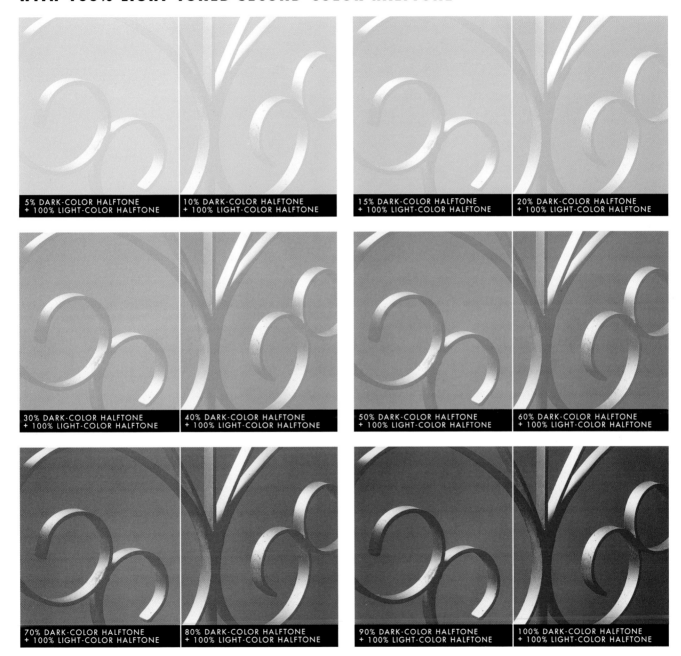

5% DARK-COLOR HALFTONE
+ 100% LIGHT-COLOR HALFTONE

10% DARK-COLOR HALFTONE
+ 100% LIGHT-COLOR HALFTONE

15% DARK-COLOR HALFTONE
+ 100% LIGHT-COLOR HALFTONE

20% DARK-COLOR HALFTONE
+ 100% LIGHT-COLOR HALFTONE

30% DARK-COLOR HALFTONE
+ 100% LIGHT-COLOR HALFTONE

40% DARK-COLOR HALFTONE
+ 100% LIGHT-COLOR HALFTONE

50% DARK-COLOR HALFTONE
+ 100% LIGHT-COLOR HALFTONE

60% DARK-COLOR HALFTONE
+ 100% LIGHT-COLOR HALFTONE

70% DARK-COLOR HALFTONE
+ 100% LIGHT-COLOR HALFTONE

80% DARK-COLOR HALFTONE
+ 100% LIGHT-COLOR HALFTONE

90% DARK-COLOR HALFTONE
+ 100% LIGHT-COLOR HALFTONE

100% DARK-COLOR HALFTONE
+ 100% LIGHT-COLOR HALFTONE

DARK-TONED HALFTONE REVERSED OUT OF/PRINTED OVER
LIGHT-TONED SECOND-COLOR FLAT TINTS OF DIFFERENT STRENGTHS

OVER 5% SECOND COLOR

OUT OF 10% SECOND COLOR

OVER 15% SECOND COLOR

OUT OF 20% SECOND COLOR

OVER 30% SECOND COLOR

OUT OF 40% SECOND COLOR

OVER 50% SECOND COLOR

OUT OF 60% SECOND COLOR

OVER 70% SECOND COLOR

OUT OF 80% SECOND COLOR

OVER 90% SECOND COLOR

OUT OF 100% SECOND COLOR

MEDIUM-TONED HALFTONE REVERSED OUT OF/PRINTED OVER DARK-TONED SECOND-COLOR FLAT TINTS OF DIFFERENT STRENGTHS

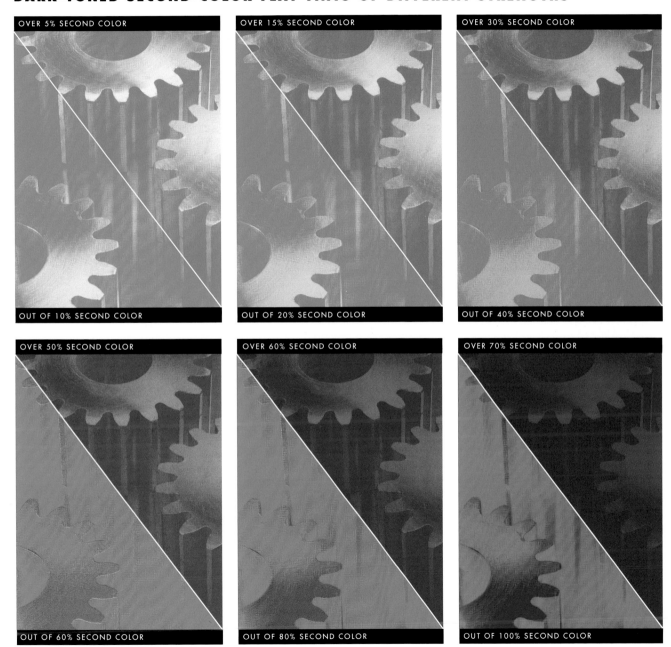

OVER 5% SECOND COLOR

OUT OF 10% SECOND COLOR

OVER 15% SECOND COLOR

OUT OF 20% SECOND COLOR

OVER 30% SECOND COLOR

OUT OF 40% SECOND COLOR

OVER 50% SECOND COLOR

OUT OF 60% SECOND COLOR

OVER 60% SECOND COLOR

OUT OF 80% SECOND COLOR

OVER 70% SECOND COLOR

OUT OF 100% SECOND COLOR

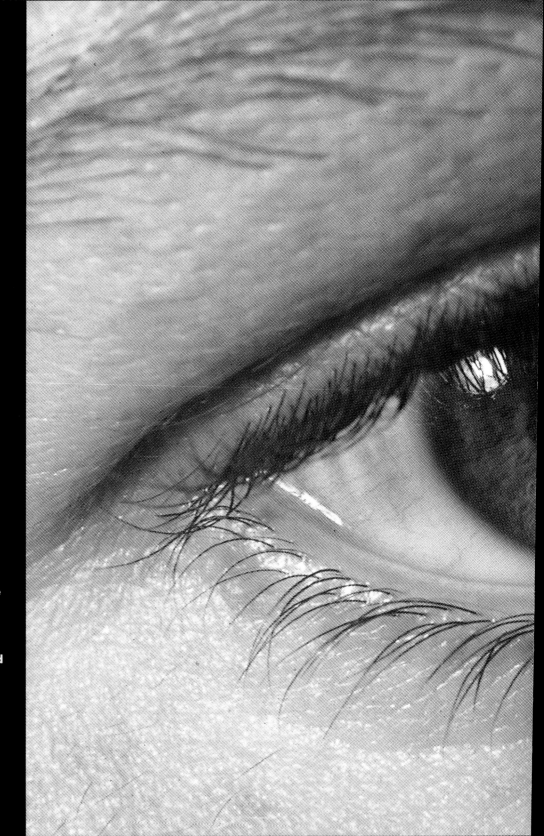

This section shows a few examples of what can be achieved by printing halftones in the four process colors — black, yellow, cyan (blue), and magenta (red).

Using these four colors mixed together in different proportions, it is possible to achieve nearly all colors. Remember that the quality and density of color is affected by the paper it is printed on and the light it is viewed by.

Colors created from the four-color process can never be as dense as single flat colors because they are created by overlapping dots. Color is subjective and there are no absolute rules. The imaginative use of the four process colors is a vital element in full-color printing, and an awareness and willingness to explore color are vital.

WORKING
WITH
FOUR
COLOR

Using this section

Working in four color can be tremendous fun and highly stimulating, but it takes a great deal of experience to be confident in using techniques imaginatively. The techniques demonstrated in this section are to be used as a springboard for creativity. The systematic examples are all clearly labeled, enabling you to give precise instructions to the printer, but of course the possible permutations are endless.

Halftone Effects is ideal for showing to clients when trying to explain a particular technique, and essential for the designer when trying to judge what the printed result will look like.

Four-color printing does not simply mean an ability to reproduce colored originals — it opens up a huge palette of color, choice, and possibilities. When marking up in four color you will need a four-color tint book. This is a color reference book that shows you the huge range of colors that can be achieved by overprinting different percentage tints from the four process colors.

Four-color reproduction and printing is often the most expensive single item involved in the production of a job. A job that goes wrong during printing can lose you a client and cost you a lot of money. When you mark up artwork or mechanicals for print, give the production house as much information as possible in a clear and precise manner. Artwork should always be double-checked by your client.

Reproduction work is often sent abroad nowadays — another reason to ensure that what you want to achieve is clearly understood. Inadequate instructions may result in reproofing, for which either you or your client will have to pay.

Below The four process colors used in this section. This section helps you to make decisions about how to use process colors.

100 90 80 70 60 50 40 30 20 10 0

PROCESS YELLOW • FADING FROM 100% TO 0%

PROCESS MAGENTA • FADING FROM 100% TO 0%

PROCESS CYAN • FADING FROM 100% TO 0%

PROCESS BLACK • FADING FROM 100% TO 0%

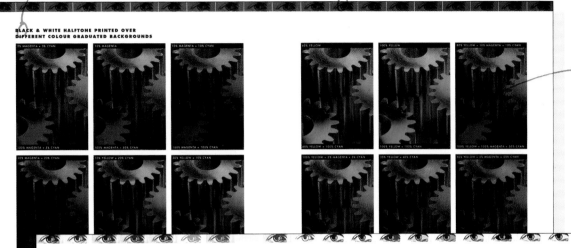

BLACK & WHITE HALFTONE PRINTED OVER DIFFERENT COLOUR GRADUATED BACKGROUNDS

4-COLOUR HALFTONE SEPARATION PRINTED WITH DIFFERENT FILM COMBINATIONS

BLACK & WHITE CUT-OUT HALFTONE PRINTED WITH DIFFERENT COLOUR BACKGROUNDS

PALE-TONED 4-COLOR HALFTONE SCANNED AT DIFFERENT STRENGTHS

4-COLOR HALFTONE • 5% STRENGTH

4-COLOR HALFTONE • 10% STRENGTH

4-COLOR HALFTONE • 15% STRENGTH

4-COLOR HALFTONE • 20% STRENGTH

4-COLOR HALFTONE • 30% STRENGTH

4-COLOR HALFTONE • 40% STRENGTH

4-COLOR HALFTONE • 50% STRENGTH

4-COLOR HALFTONE • 60% STRENGTH

4-COLOR HALFTONE • 70% STRENGTH

4-COLOR HALFTONE • 80% STRENGTH

4-COLOR HALFTONE • 90% STRENGTH

4-COLOR HALFTONE • 100% STRENGTH

MEDIUM-TONED 4-COLOR HALFTONE SCANNED AT DIFFERENT STRENGTHS

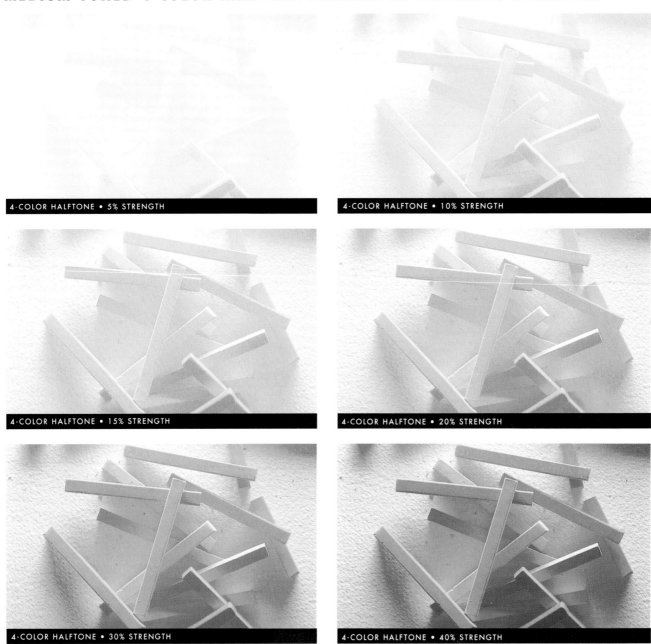

4-COLOR HALFTONE • 5% STRENGTH

4-COLOR HALFTONE • 10% STRENGTH

4-COLOR HALFTONE • 15% STRENGTH

4-COLOR HALFTONE • 20% STRENGTH

4-COLOR HALFTONE • 30% STRENGTH

4-COLOR HALFTONE • 40% STRENGTH

4-COLOR HALFTONE • 50% STRENGTH

4-COLOR HALFTONE • 60% STRENGTH

4-COLOR HALFTONE • 70% STRENGTH

4-COLOR HALFTONE • 80% STRENGTH

4-COLOR HALFTONE • 90% STRENGTH

4-COLOR HALFTONE • 100% STRENGTH

STRONG-TONED 4-COLOR HALFTONE SCANNED AT DIFFERENT STRENGTHS

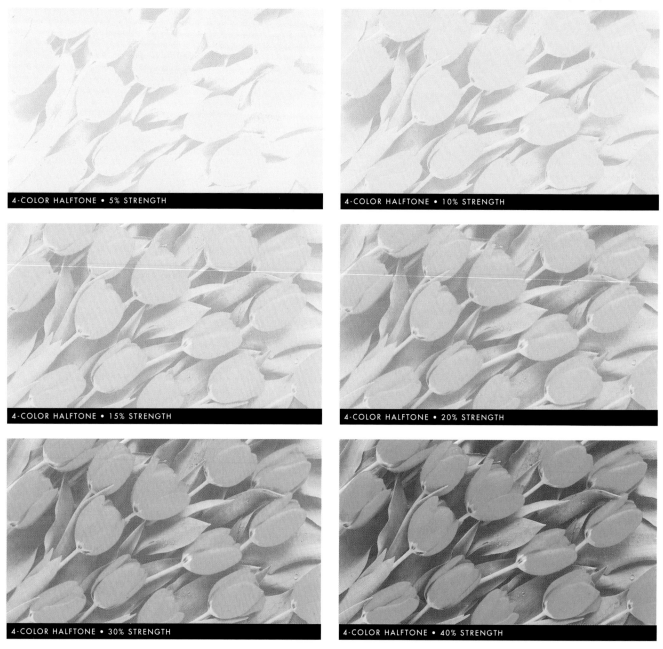

4-COLOR HALFTONE • 5% STRENGTH

4-COLOR HALFTONE • 10% STRENGTH

4-COLOR HALFTONE • 15% STRENGTH

4-COLOR HALFTONE • 20% STRENGTH

4-COLOR HALFTONE • 30% STRENGTH

4-COLOR HALFTONE • 40% STRENGTH

4-COLOR HALFTONE • 50% STRENGTH

4-COLOR HALFTONE • 60% STRENGTH

4-COLOR HALFTONE • 70% STRENGTH

4-COLOR HALFTONE • 80% STRENGTH

4-COLOR HALFTONE • 90% STRENGTH

4-COLOR HALFTONE • 100% STRENGTH

BLACK & WHITE HALFTONE
SCANNED IN 4-COLOR AT DIFFERENT SCREEN SIZES

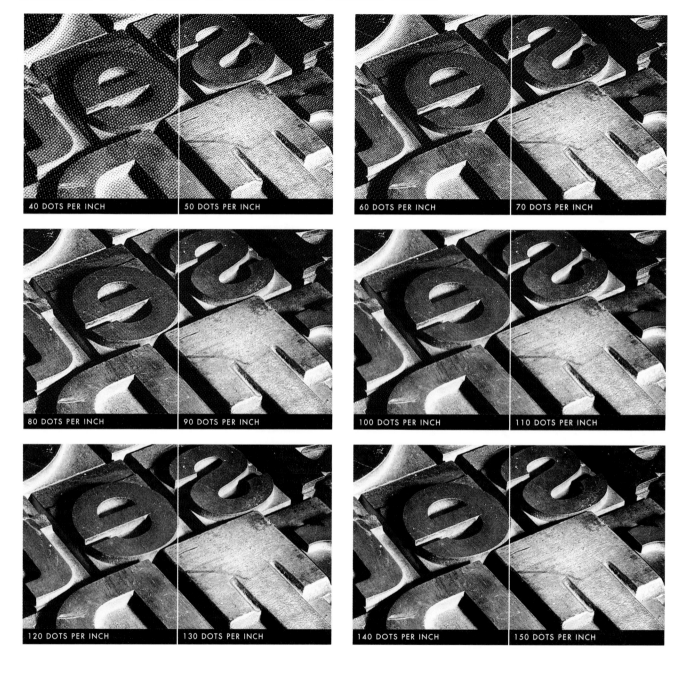

40 DOTS PER INCH | 50 DOTS PER INCH | 60 DOTS PER INCH | 70 DOTS PER INCH
80 DOTS PER INCH | 90 DOTS PER INCH | 100 DOTS PER INCH | 110 DOTS PER INCH
120 DOTS PER INCH | 130 DOTS PER INCH | 140 DOTS PER INCH | 150 DOTS PER INCH

4-COLOR HALFTONE SCANNED AT DIFFERENT SCREEN SIZES

40 DOTS PER INCH

50 DOTS PER INCH

60 DOTS PER INCH

70 DOTS PER INCH

80 DOTS PER INCH

90 DOTS PER INCH

100 DOTS PER INCH

110 DOTS PER INCH

120 DOTS PER INCH

130 DOTS PER INCH

140 DOTS PER INCH

150 DOTS PER INCH

BLACK & WHITE HALFTONE PRINTED IN DIFFERENT 4-COLOR MIXES

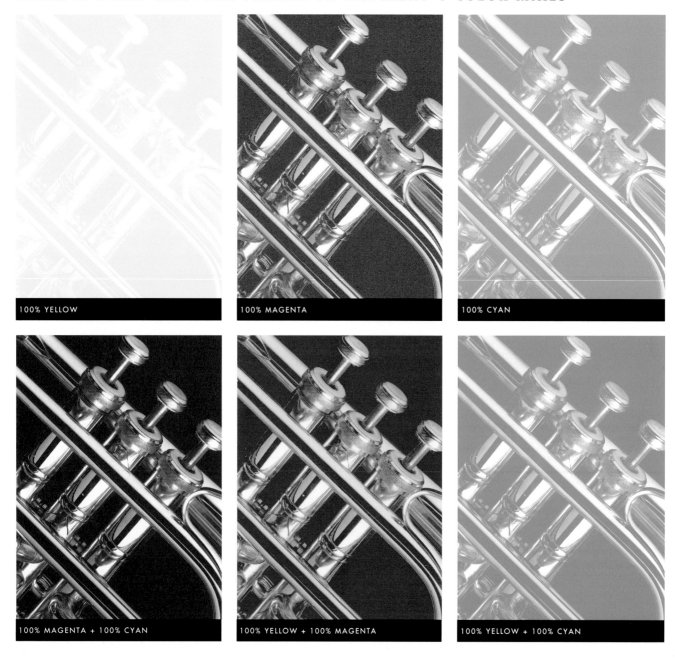

100% YELLOW

100% MAGENTA

100% CYAN

100% MAGENTA + 100% CYAN

100% YELLOW + 100% MAGENTA

100% YELLOW + 100% CYAN

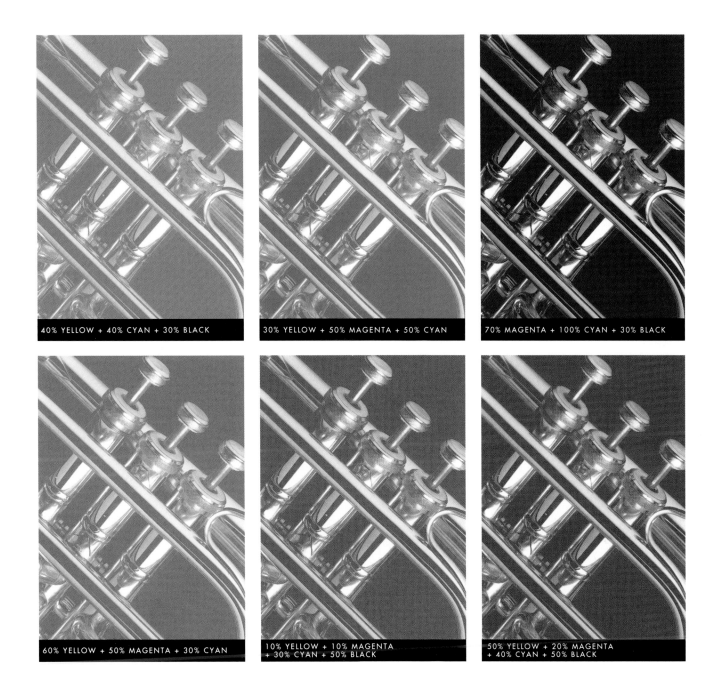

40% YELLOW + 40% CYAN + 30% BLACK

30% YELLOW + 50% MAGENTA + 50% CYAN

70% MAGENTA + 100% CYAN + 30% BLACK

60% YELLOW + 50% MAGENTA + 30% CYAN

10% YELLOW + 10% MAGENTA
+ 30% CYAN + 50% BLACK

50% YELLOW + 20% MAGENTA
+ 40% CYAN + 50% BLACK

4-COLOR HALFTONE SEPARATION
PRINTED WITH DIFFERENT FILM COMBINATIONS

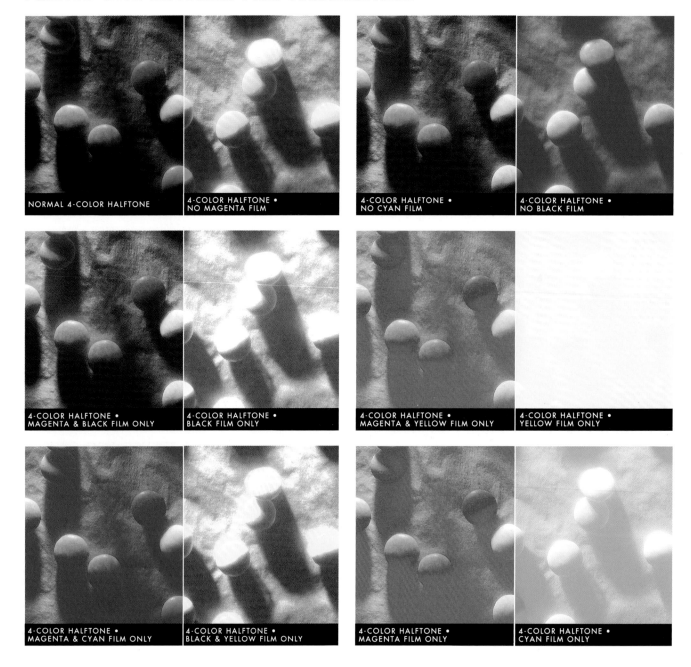

NORMAL 4-COLOR HALFTONE

4-COLOR HALFTONE •
NO MAGENTA FILM

4-COLOR HALFTONE •
NO CYAN FILM

4-COLOR HALFTONE •
NO BLACK FILM

4-COLOR HALFTONE •
MAGENTA & BLACK FILM ONLY

4-COLOR HALFTONE •
BLACK FILM ONLY

4-COLOR HALFTONE •
MAGENTA & YELLOW FILM ONLY

4-COLOR HALFTONE •
YELLOW FILM ONLY

4-COLOR HALFTONE •
MAGENTA & CYAN FILM ONLY

4-COLOR HALFTONE •
BLACK & YELLOW FILM ONLY

4-COLOR HALFTONE •
MAGENTA FILM ONLY

4-COLOR HALFTONE •
CYAN FILM ONLY

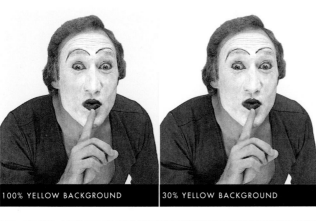

BLACK & WHITE SILHOUETTE HALFTONE
PRINTED WITH DIFFERENT COLOR BACKGROUNDS

100% YELLOW BACKGROUND

30% YELLOW BACKGROUND

100% MAGENTA BACKGROUND

30% MAGENTA BACKGROUND

100% CYAN BACKGROUND

30% CYAN BACKGROUND

100% BLACK BACKGROUND

30% BLACK BACKGROUND

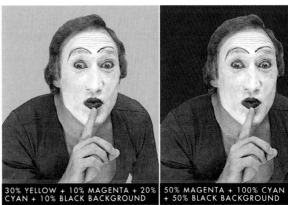

30% YELLOW + 20% MAGENTA + 20% CYAN BACKGROUND

10% YELLOW + 30% MAGENTA + 50% CYAN BACKGROUND

30% YELLOW + 10% MAGENTA + 20% CYAN + 10% BLACK BACKGROUND

50% MAGENTA + 100% CYAN + 50% BLACK BACKGROUND

TRANSPOSING AND PRINTING 2 FILMS ONLY FROM A 4-COLOR SEPARATION

NORMAL 4-COLOR HALFTONE

BLACK FILM PRINTED MAGENTA + MAGENTA FILM PRINTED BLACK

BLACK FILM PRINTED CYAN + CYAN FILM PRINTED BLACK

YELLOW FILM PRINTED MAGENTA + MAGENTA FILM PRINTED YELLOW

BLACK FILM PRINTED YELLOW + CYAN FILM PRINTED MAGENTA

CYAN FILM PRINTED YELLOW + MAGENTA FILM PRINTED BLACK

YELLOW FILM PRINTED CYAN + MAGENTA FILM PRINTED BLACK

MAGENTA FILM PRINTED YELLOW + BLACK FILM PRINTED CYAN

YELLOW FILM PRINTED BLACK + MAGENTA FILM PRINTED YELLOW

CYAN FILM PRINTED BLACK + MAGENTA FILM PRINTED CYAN

MAGENTA FILM PRINTED BLACK + YELLOW FILM PRINTED CYAN

CYAN FILM PRINTED YELLOW + MAGENTA FILM PRINTED CYAN

BLACK & WHITE HALFTONE PRINTED OVER DIFFERENT COLOR BACKGROUNDS

OVER 20% YELLOW

OVER 20% YELLOW + 10% MAGENTA

OVER 20% YELLOW + 20% MAGENTA

OVER 20% YELLOW
+ 10% MAGENTA + 10% CYAN

OVER 20% YELLOW
+10% MAGENTA + 20% CYAN

OVER 20% YELLOW + 20% CYAN

OVER 20% YELLOW
+ 20% MAGENTA + 20% CYAN

OVER 10% CYAN

OVER 10% MAGENTA + 10% CYAN

OVER 10% MAGENTA + 20% CYAN

OVER 20% MAGENTA + 20% CYAN

OVER 10% YELLOW
+ 10% MAGENTA + 20% CYAN

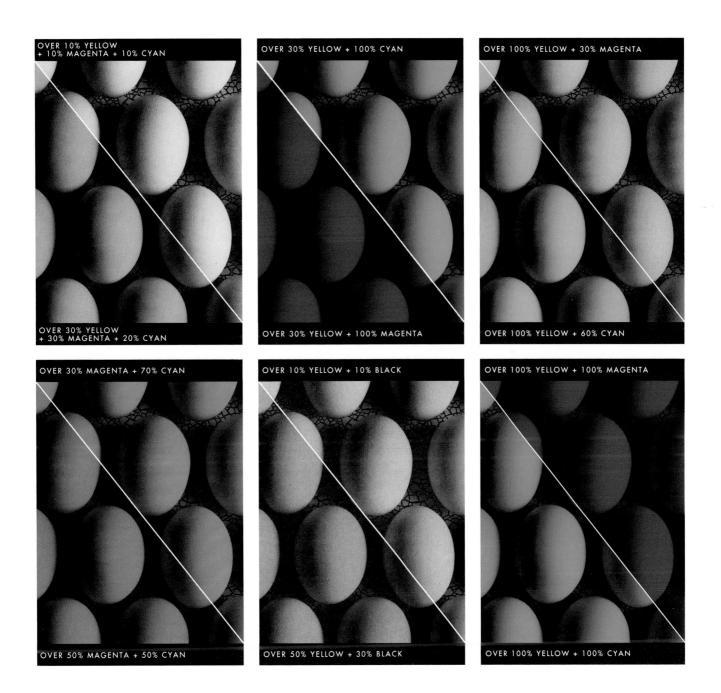

OVER 10% YELLOW
+ 10% MAGENTA + 10% CYAN

OVER 30% YELLOW + 100% CYAN

OVER 100% YELLOW + 30% MAGENTA

OVER 30% YELLOW
+ 30% MAGENTA + 20% CYAN

OVER 30% YELLOW + 100% MAGENTA

OVER 100% YELLOW + 60% CYAN

OVER 30% MAGENTA + 70% CYAN

OVER 10% YELLOW + 10% BLACK

OVER 100% YELLOW + 100% MAGENTA

OVER 50% MAGENTA + 50% CYAN

OVER 50% YELLOW + 30% BLACK

OVER 100% YELLOW + 100% CYAN

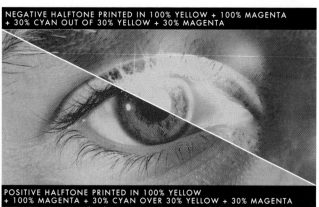

BLACK & WHITE HALFTONE PRINTED IN DIFFERENT 4-COLOR MIXES, OVER DIFFERENT COLOR BACKGROUNDS

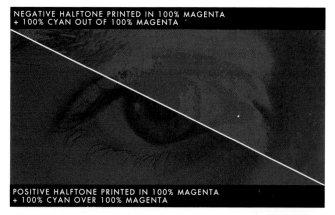

NEGATIVE HALFTONE PRINTED IN 100% MAGENTA + 100% CYAN OUT OF 100% MAGENTA

POSITIVE HALFTONE PRINTED IN 100% MAGENTA + 100% CYAN OVER 100% MAGENTA

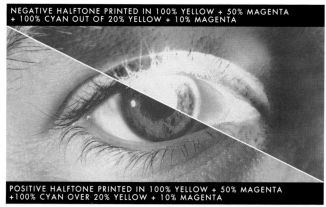

NEGATIVE HALFTONE PRINTED IN 100% YELLOW + 50% MAGENTA + 100% CYAN OUT OF 20% YELLOW + 10% MAGENTA

POSITIVE HALFTONE PRINTED IN 100% YELLOW + 50% MAGENTA + 100% CYAN OVER 20% YELLOW + 10% MAGENTA

NEGATIVE HALFTONE PRINTED IN 100% YELLOW + 100% MAGENTA + 30% CYAN OUT OF 30% YELLOW + 30% MAGENTA

POSITIVE HALFTONE PRINTED IN 100% YELLOW + 100% MAGENTA + 30% CYAN OVER 30% YELLOW + 30% MAGENTA

NEGATIVE HALFTONE PRINTED IN 50% MAGENTA + 100% CYAN OUT OF 10% MAGENTA + 20% CYAN

POSITIVE HALFTONE PRINTED IN 50% MAGENTA + 100% CYAN OVER 10% MAGENTA + 20% CYAN

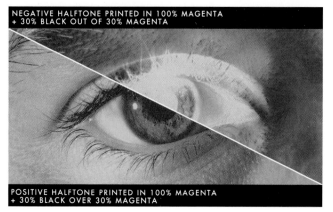

NEGATIVE HALFTONE PRINTED IN 100% MAGENTA + 30% BLACK OUT OF 30% MAGENTA

POSITIVE HALFTONE PRINTED IN 100% MAGENTA + 30% BLACK OVER 30% MAGENTA

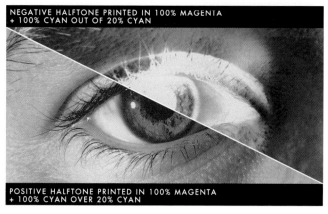

NEGATIVE HALFTONE PRINTED IN 100% MAGENTA + 100% CYAN OUT OF 20% CYAN

POSITIVE HALFTONE PRINTED IN 100% MAGENTA + 100% CYAN OVER 20% CYAN

NEGATIVE HALFTONE PRINTED IN 100% YELLOW + 100% MAGENTA + 50% CYAN OUT OF 20% YELLOW + 10% MAGENTA + 10% CYAN

POSITIVE HALFTONE PRINTED IN 100% YELLOW + 100% MAGENTA + 50% CYAN OVER 20% YELLOW + 10% MAGENTA + 10% CYAN

NEGATIVE HALFTONE PRINTED IN 100% YELLOW + 50% MAGENTA + 100% CYAN OUT OF 20% YELLOW + 10% CYAN

POSITIVE HALFTONE PRINTED IN 100% YELLOW + 50% MAGENTA + 100% CYAN OVER 20% YELLOW + 10% CYAN

NEGATIVE HALFTONE PRINTED IN 100% MAGENTA + 100% CYAN + 50% BLACK OUT OF 10% MAGENTA

POSITIVE HALFTONE PRINTED IN 100% MAGENTA + 100% CYAN + 50% BLACK OVER 10% MAGENTA

NEGATIVE HALFTONE PRINTED IN 100% YELLOW + 100% MAGENTA + 100% BLACK OUT OF 20% YELLOW + 10% MAGENTA

POSITIVE HALFTONE PRINTED IN 100% YELLOW + 100% MAGENTA + 100% BLACK OVER 20% YELLOW + 10% MAGENTA

NEGATIVE HALFTONE PRINTED IN 100% YELLOW + 100% MAGENTA OUT OF 20% YELLOW

POSITIVE HALFTONE PRINTED IN 100% YELLOW + 100% MAGENTA OVER 20% YELLOW

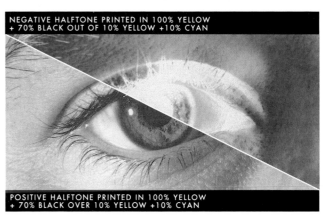

NEGATIVE HALFTONE PRINTED IN 100% YELLOW + 70% BLACK OUT OF 10% YELLOW +10% CYAN

POSITIVE HALFTONE PRINTED IN 100% YELLOW + 70% BLACK OVER 10% YELLOW +10% CYAN

BLACK & WHITE HALFTONE PRINTED OVER
DIFFERENT COLOR GRADATED BACKGROUNDS

5% MAGENTA + 5% CYAN

100% MAGENTA + 5% CYAN

10% MAGENTA

100% MAGENTA + 50% CYAN

10% MAGENTA + 10% CYAN

100% MAGENTA + 100% CYAN

10% MAGENTA + 20% CYAN

100% MAGENTA + 100% CYAN

10% YELLOW + 20% CYAN

10% YELLOW + 50% MAGENTA + 100% CYAN

30% YELLOW + 10% CYAN

30% YELLOW + 20% MAGENTA + 100% CYAN

60% YELLOW

60% YELLOW + 100% CYAN

100% YELLOW

100% YELLOW + 100% CYAN

80% YELLOW + 10% MAGENTA + 10% CYAN

100% YELLOW + 100% MAGENTA + 50% CYAN

100% YELLOW + 5% MAGENTA + 5% CYAN

100% YELLOW + 100% MAGENTA + 5% CYAN

30% YELLOW + 40% CYAN

30% YELLOW + 100% MAGENTA + 40% CYAN

50% YELLOW + 5% MAGENTA + 55% CYAN

50% YELLOW + 100% MAGENTA + 15% CYAN

BLACK & WHITE HALFTONE SCANNED IN 4 COLORS • RED

50% BLACK HALFTONE + 50% MAGENTA HALFTONE

100% BLACK HALFTONE + 50% MAGENTA HALFTONE

50% BLACK HALFTONE + 100% MAGENTA + 30% CYAN HALFTONE

100% BLACK HALFTONE + 100% MAGENTA + 30% CYAN HALFTONE

50% BLACK HALFTONE + 50% YELLOW
+ 100% MAGENTA + 30% CYAN HALFTONE

100% BLACK HALFTONE + 50% YELLOW
+ 100% MAGENTA + 30% CYAN HALFTONE

50% BLACK HALFTONE + 30% YELLOW + 100% MAGENTA HALFTONE

100% BLACK HALFTONE + 30% YELLOW + 100% MAGENTA HALFTONE

50% BLACK HALFTONE + 50% YELLOW + 50% MAGENTA HALFTONE

100% BLACK HALFTONE + 50% YELLOW + 50% MAGENTA HALFTONE

50% BLACK HALFTONE + 100% YELLOW + 100% MAGENTA HALFTONE

100% BLACK HALFTONE + 100% YELLOW + 100% MAGENTA HALFTONE

BLACK & WHITE HALFTONE SCANNED IN 4 COLORS · SEPIA

50% BLACK HALFTONE + 50% YELLOW + 70% MAGENTA HALFTONE

100% BLACK HALFTONE + 50% YELLOW + 70% MAGENTA HALFTONE

50% BLACK HALFTONE + 100% YELLOW + 70% MAGENTA HALFTONE

100% BLACK HALFTONE + 100% YELLOW + 70% MAGENTA HALFTONE

50% BLACK HALFTONE + 70% YELLOW + 70% MAGENTA HALFTONE

100% BLACK HALFTONE + 70% YELLOW + 70% MAGENTA HALFTONE

50% BLACK HALFTONE + 50% YELLOW + 50% MAGENTA HALFTONE

100% BLACK HALFTONE + 50% YELLOW + 50% MAGENTA HALFTONE

50% BLACK HALFTONE + 100% YELLOW + 50% MAGENTA HALFTONE

100% BLACK HALFTONE + 100% YELLOW + 50% MAGENTA HALFTONE

50% BLACK HALFTONE + 70% YELLOW + 40% MAGENTA HALFTONE

100% BLACK HALFTONE + 70% YELLOW + 40% MAGENTA HALFTONE

BLACK & WHITE HALFTONE SCANNED IN 4 COLORS • BLUE

50% BLACK HALFTONE
+ 100% CYAN HALFTONE

100% BLACK HALFTONE
+ 100% CYAN HALFTONE

50% BLACK HALFTONE
+ 50% CYAN HALFTONE

100% BLACK HALFTONE
+ 50% CYAN HALFTONE

50% BLACK HALFTONE
+ 50% MANGENTA + 100% CYAN HALFTONE

100% BLACK HALFTONE
+ 50% MAGENTA + 100% CYAN HALFTONE

50% BLACK HALFTONE
+ 15% MAGENTA + 50% CYAN HALFTONE

100% BLACK HALFTONE
+ 15% MAGENTA + 50% CYAN HALFTONE

50% BLACK HALFTONE
+ 30% MAGENTA + 100% CYAN HALFTONE

100% BLACK HALFTONE
+ 30% MAGENTA + 100% CYAN HALFTONE

50% BLACK HALFTONE
+ 70% MAGENTA + 100% CYAN HALFTONE

100% BLACK HALFTONE
+ 70% MAGENTA + 100% CYAN HALFTONE

BLACK & WHITE HALFTONE SCANNED IN 4 COLORS • PURPLE

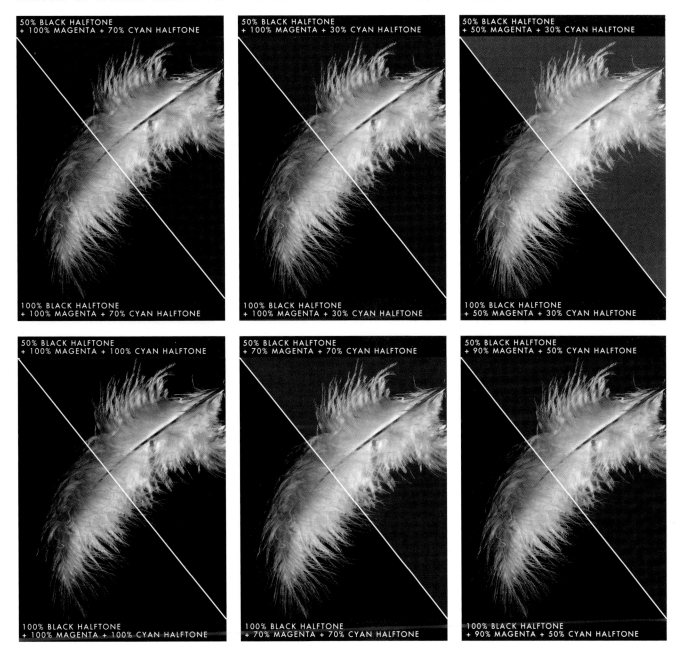

50% BLACK HALFTONE
+ 100% MAGENTA + 70% CYAN HALFTONE

100% BLACK HALFTONE
+ 100% MAGENTA + 70% CYAN HALFTONE

50% BLACK HALFTONE
+ 100% MAGENTA + 30% CYAN HALFTONE

100% BLACK HALFTONE
+ 100% MAGENTA + 30% CYAN HALFTONE

50% BLACK HALFTONE
+ 50% MAGENTA + 30% CYAN HALFTONE

100% BLACK HALFTONE
+ 50% MAGENTA + 30% CYAN HALFTONE

50% BLACK HALFTONE
+ 100% MAGENTA + 100% CYAN HALFTONE

100% BLACK HALFTONE
+ 100% MAGENTA + 100% CYAN HALFTONE

50% BLACK HALFTONE
+ 70% MAGENTA + 70% CYAN HALFTONE

100% BLACK HALFTONE
+ 70% MAGENTA + 70% CYAN HALFTONE

50% BLACK HALFTONE
+ 90% MAGENTA + 50% CYAN HALFTONE

100% BLACK HALFTONE
+ 90% MAGENTA + 50% CYAN HALFTONE

BLACK & WHITE HALFTONE SCANNED IN 4 COLORS • GREEN

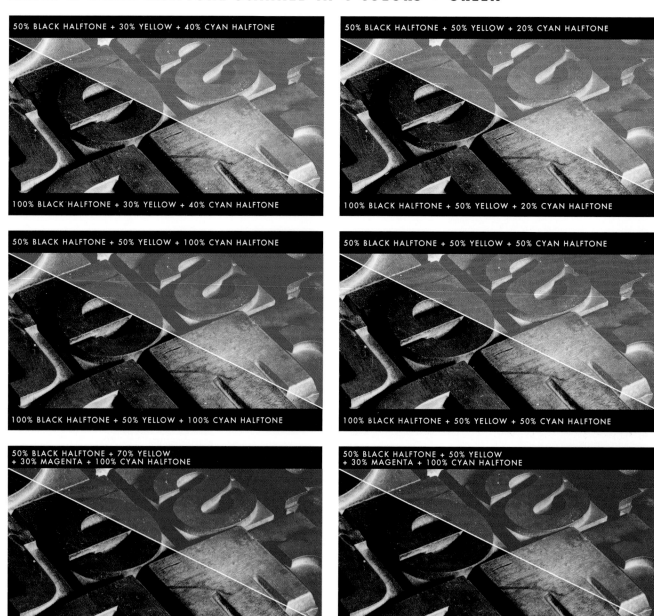

50% BLACK HALFTONE + 30% YELLOW + 40% CYAN HALFTONE

100% BLACK HALFTONE + 30% YELLOW + 40% CYAN HALFTONE

50% BLACK HALFTONE + 50% YELLOW + 20% CYAN HALFTONE

100% BLACK HALFTONE + 50% YELLOW + 20% CYAN HALFTONE

50% BLACK HALFTONE + 50% YELLOW + 100% CYAN HALFTONE

100% BLACK HALFTONE + 50% YELLOW + 100% CYAN HALFTONE

50% BLACK HALFTONE + 50% YELLOW + 50% CYAN HALFTONE

100% BLACK HALFTONE + 50% YELLOW + 50% CYAN HALFTONE

50% BLACK HALFTONE + 70% YELLOW
+ 30% MAGENTA + 100% CYAN HALFTONE

100% BLACK HALFTONE + 70% YELLOW
+ 30% MAGENTA + 100% CYAN HALFTONE

50% BLACK HALFTONE + 50% YELLOW
+ 30% MAGENTA + 100% CYAN HALFTONE

100% BLACK HALFTONE + 50% YELLOW
+ 30% MAGENTA + 100% CYAN HALFTONE

BLACK & WHITE HALFTONE SCANNED IN 4 COLORS • YELLOW

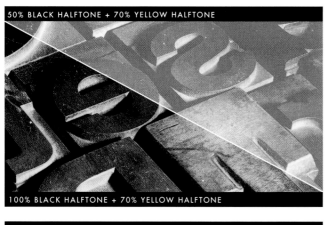

50% BLACK HALFTONE + 70% YELLOW HALFTONE

100% BLACK HALFTONE + 70% YELLOW HALFTONE

50% BLACK HALFTONE + 40% YELLOW HALFTONE

100% BLACK HALFTONE + 40% YELLOW HALFTONE

50% BLACK HALFTONE + 100% YELLOW + 30% MAGENTA HALFTONE

100% BLACK HALFTONE + 100% YELLOW + 30% MAGENTA HALFTONE

50% BLACK HALFTONE + 50% YELLOW + 30% MAGENTA HALFTONE

100% BLACK HALFTONE + 50% YELLOW + 30% MAGENTA HALFTONE

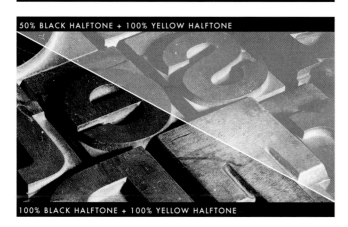

50% BLACK HALFTONE + 100% YELLOW HALFTONE

100% BLACK HALFTONE + 100% YELLOW HALFTONE

50% BLACK HALFTONE + 70% YELLOW + 10% MAGENTA HALFTONE

100% BLACK HALFTONE + 70% YELLOW + 10% MAGENTA HALFTONE

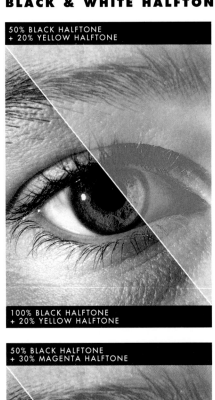

BLACK & WHITE HALFTONE SCANNED IN 4 COLORS • PASTELS

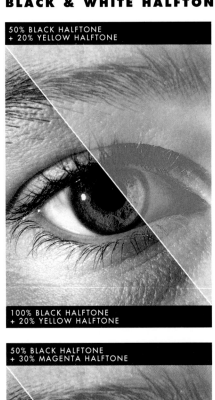
50% BLACK HALFTONE
+ 20% YELLOW HALFTONE

100% BLACK HALFTONE
+ 20% YELLOW HALFTONE

50% BLACK HALFTONE
+ 10% YELLOW + 10% MAGENTA HALFTONE

100% BLACK HALFTONE
+ 10% YELLOW + 10% MAGENTA HALFTONE

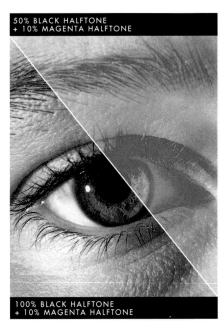
50% BLACK HALFTONE
+ 10% MAGENTA HALFTONE

100% BLACK HALFTONE
+ 10% MAGENTA HALFTONE

50% BLACK HALFTONE
+ 30% MAGENTA HALFTONE

100% BLACK HALFTONE
+ 30% MAGENTA HALFTONE

50% BLACK HALFTONE
+ 10% MAGENTA + 10% CYAN HALFTONE

100% BLACK HALFTONE
+ 10% MAGENTA + 10% CYAN HALFTONE

50% BLACK HALFTONE
+ 20% MAGENTA + 10% CYAN HALFTONE

100% BLACK HALFTONE
+ 20% MAGENTA + 10% CYAN HALFTONE

50% BLACK HALFTONE
+ 30% MAGENTA HALFTONE

100% BLACK HALFTONE
+ 30% MAGENTA HALFTONE

50% BLACK HALFTONE
+ 20% MAGENTA + 20% CYAN HALFTONE

100% BLACK HALFTONE
+ 20% MAGENTA + 20% CYAN HALFTONE

50% BLACK HALFTONE
+ 10% CYAN HALFTONE

100% BLACK HALFTONE
+ 10% CYAN HALFTONE

50% BLACK HALFTONE
+ 20% CYAN HALFTONE

100% BLACK HALFTONE
+ 20% CYAN HALFTONE

50% BLACK HALFTONE
+ 20% YELLOW + 20% CYAN HALFTONE

100% BLACK HALFTONE
+ 20% YELLOW + 20% CYAN HALFTONE

50% BLACK HALFTONE
+ 30% YELLOW + 40% CYAN HALFTONE

100% BLACK HALFTONE
+ 30% YELLOW + 40% CYAN HALFTONE

This section deals with half-tones that are treated graphically to create a different visual interpretation from the original.

When requesting special effects, remember that they can be unpredictable and expensive to produce.

Computerized manipulation and electronic imagery can be exciting and surprising, but never hope that a special effect will disguise lack of creativity.

WORKING WITH SPECIAL EFFECTS

Black and white line effects

All special effects offer the designer the possibility of creating a different interpretation of the original to produce a greater visual impact. The simple line conversion technique is a process of converting a continuous-tone photograph into a line illustration. A high-contrast lithography film is used, which eliminates all the intermediate tones in the original photograph. Because there are no intermediate tones, one should try to visualize in advance how an image will work.

The tone-line technique is a process sometimes used to produce a more tentative image. The effect achieved is that of a pen-and-ink drawing, but it is produced by purely photographic means. It works particularly well when fine detail is required. The linear quality is produced by using a continuous-tone film negative and a continuous-tone positive mask of equal density. The positive and negative tones cancel each other out except at the edges of the image, producing a distinct line image.

The one-way halftone screen reproduces the original in a series of horizontal lines that swell and contract to form the shadows and highlights. The effect is of an engraved line.

All of these line effects can be used in a variety of ways – the line image can be printed as a negative, overprinted on solid color or a screen tint, or the same image can be repeated out of register.

Marking up

Originals should be sharp, well-balanced, and have good contrast. The process of converting halftone to line inevitably leads to loss of detail, but this is usually balanced by the graphic effect created.

LINE CONVERSION • HORIZONTAL LINE SCREEN

LINE CONVERSION • HIGH CONTRAST FILM

LINE CONVERSION • WAVY LINE SCREEN

LINE CONVERSION • CONCENTRIC CIRCLE SCREEN

LINE CONVERSION • COARSE MEZZOTINT

LINE CONVERSION • ONE-WAY SCREEN

Duotones using the process colors

The duotone process is not a technique that the designer would use for everyday jobs. However, as a means of achieving image enhancement it gives that extra quality sometimes required.

The duotone process is a special effect that requires two halftones made to different screen angles from the same copy. One plate is usually printed in black and the other in gray or a second color. Two black printings are used to give greater depth and detail to the image than would be possible with a single halftone plate. To achieve this, one plate is made to render the highlights, the other to bring out details in the shadow. When the two plates are printed in register an extra dimension is created.

If a second color is used on the highlight plate, the photographic image will look as though it has been tinted. The designer may not want the full strength of the second color, and can ask for it to be printed at a different strength. Certain color combinations can be used to considerable effect.

There are a number of variations on the duotone idea, which, though not strictly duotones, are nevertheless useful effects; for example, printing a normal halftone on a colored paper, or overprinted onto a screen tint. A normal halftone can also be printed twice; once in color and once in black. If the images are slightly out of register, a kind of duotone effect is created.

Marking up

Many duotones are marked up from the four process colors. Write clearly that the halftone is to be reproduced as a duotone, and then specify the two colors and their respective percentage strengths.

DUOTONE • 100% BLACK HALFTONE + 100% CYAN HALFTONE

DUOTONE • 100% BLACK HALFTONE + 30% CYAN HALFTONE

DUOTONE • 50% BLACK HALFTONE + 100% CYAN HALFTONE

DUOTONE • 100% BLACK HALFTONE + 100% MAGENTA HALFTONE

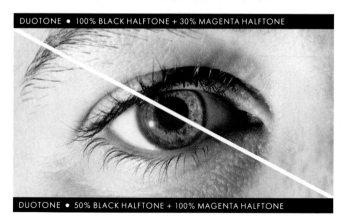

DUOTONE • 100% BLACK HALFTONE + 30% MAGENTA HALFTONE

DUOTONE • 50% BLACK HALFTONE + 100% MAGENTA HALFTONE

DUOTONE • 100% BLACK HALFTONE + 100% YELLOW HALFTONE

DUOTONE • 100% BLACK HALFTONE + 30% YELLOW HALFTONE

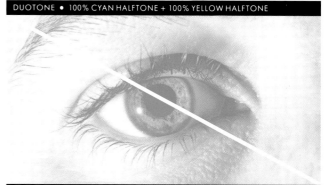

DUOTONE • 100% CYAN HALFTONE + 100% YELLOW HALFTONE

DUOTONE • 100% CYAN HALFTONE + 30% YELLOW HALFTONE

DUOTONE • 50% BLACK HALFTONE + 100% YELLOW HALFTONE

DUOTONE • 100% CYAN HALFTONE + 100% MAGENTA HALFTONE

DUOTONE • 50% CYAN HALFTONE + 100% YELLOW HALFTONE

DUOTONE • 50% MAGENTA HALFTONE + 100% CYAN HALFTONE

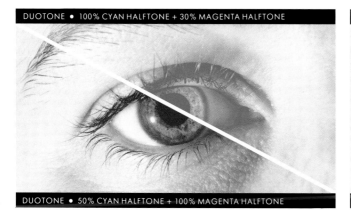

DUOTONE • 100% CYAN HALFTONE + 30% MAGENTA HALFTONE

DUOTONE • 50% CYAN HALFTONE + 100% MAGENTA HALFTONE

DUOTONE • 100% MAGENTA HALFTONE + 30% CYAN HALFTONE

DUOTONE • 50% YELLOW HALFTONE + 100% MAGENTA HALFTONE

Overprinting type on images

Legibility of type is an essential element in most printed graphics. Being able to judge success-fully whether type will be clear when printed over or reversed out of a photograph is a matter of judgment.

Pictures usually have varying degrees of tone and color within them, and a block of text which reverses well out of one part of an image may be totally illegible elsewhere. As it is not always possible to choose the ideal picture to use in conjunction with type, it is sometimes necessary to apply techniques which improve clarity.

Color and tone can be introduced into type in order to make it stand out against an image. It is also possible to lay areas of tint over an image in order to make type more legible. In book production there are often co-editions with foreign publishers and these can be economical if the black plate alone is changed. If type is reversed out of one or more of the other colors, this would involve changing extra plates which could make the co-edition uneconomical. Reversing type out of black or gray areas within a picture can save a client money.

Marking up

If you are in doubt about legibility of type, make a mock-up of your design before you send your artwork to a printer. Areas of color to be laid over or reversed out of a picture need to be indicated on a precise overlay. If you are adding tinted panels to four-color pictures you need to discuss with your printer how to avoid moiré. Usually the answer is to delete the panel color from that area of the picture which is to have the panel.

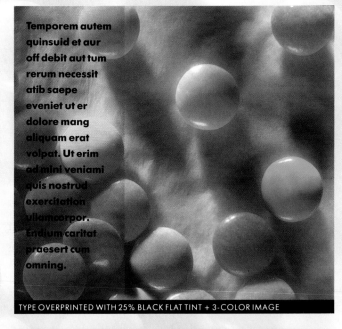

Temporem autem quinsuid et aur off debit aut tum rerum necessit atib saepe eveniet ut er dolore mang aliquam erat volpat. Ut erim ad mini veniami quis nostrud exercitation ullamcorpor. Endium caritat praesert cum omning.

TYPE OVERPRINTED WITH 25% BLACK FLAT TINT + 3-COLOR IMAGE

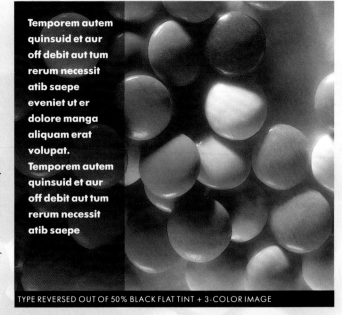

Temporem autem quinsuid et aur off debit aut tum rerum necessit atib saepe eveniet ut er dolore manga aliquam erat volupat. Temporem autem quinsuid et aur off debit aut tum rerum necessit atib saepe

TYPE REVERSED OUT OF 50% BLACK FLAT TINT + 3-COLOR IMAGE

Ut erim ad mini veniami quis. Temporem autem quinsuid et aur off debit aut tum rerum necessit atib eveniet ut er dolore mang aliquam erat volpat. Temporem autem

Er dolore mang aliquam erat volpat. Temporem autem quinsuid et aur off debit aut tum rerum necessit atib saepe eveniet ut er dolore mang aliquam erat volpat. Ut erim ad mini

TYPE PRINTED OVER + REVERSED OUT OF AN IMAGE

Rerum necessit atib saepe eveniet ut er dolore manga aliquam erat volupat. Temporem autem quinsuid et aur off debit aut tum rerum necessit atib saepe eveniet ut er

TYPE PRINTED OVER 10% GHOSTED AREA

Mang aliquam erat volpat. Temporem aute quinsuid et aur off debit aut tum rerum necessit atib saepe eveniet ut er dolore mang aliquam erat volpat. Ut erim ad mini

TYPE REVERSED OUT OF 100% MAGENTA

Debit aut tum rerum necessit atib saepe eveniet ut er dolore manga aliquam erat volupat. Temporem autem quinsuid et aur off debit aut tum rerum necessit atib saepe

TYPE PRINTED OUT OF 100% BLACK

Eveniet ut er dolore mang aliquam erat volpat. Temporem autem quinsuid et aur off debit aut tum rerum necessit atib saepe eveniet ut er dolore mang aliquam erat volpat.

TYPE REVERSED OUT OF 50% CYAN + 3-COLOR IMAGE

Manga aliquam erat volupat. Temporem autem quinsuid et aur off debit aut tum rerum necessit atib saepe eveniet ut er dolore mang aliquam erat volpat. Temporem

TYPE REVERSED OUT OF 30% BLACK + 3-COLOR IMAGE

Horizontal distortion

A designer generally uses a distorted image to create a sense of movement, to prevent a page-layout looking too static. A distorted image always refers to its original state, but we are aware that it has been stretched, compressed, twisted, or bent. When we look at a landscape scene, for instance, we have an idea of what it ought to look like from past experience of other landscapes. If, however, that same scene is stretched photographically, the horizontal values are exaggerated.

The placement of such an image on the page is critical to the balance of the layout. For example, a landscape might work better at the bottom of a spread than at the top, because of the sense of gravity associated with the subject.

Marking up

The horizontal stretching of an image is specified by percentage. This technique ensures that the image is enlarged to a greater degree horizontally than it is vertically.

SILHOUETTE 4-COLOR HALFTONE

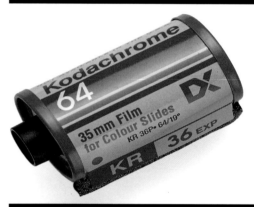

SILHOUETTE 4-COLOR HALFTONE • STRETCHED 120%

SILHOUETTE 4-COLOR HALFTONE • STRETCHED 140%

SILHOUETTE 4-COLOR HALFTONE • STRETCHED 160%

SILHOUETTE 4-COLOR HALFTONE • STRETCHED 220%

SILHOUETTE 4-COLOR HALFTONE • STRETCHED 180%

SILHOUETTE 4-COLOR HALFTONE • STRETCHED 240%

SILHOUETTE 4-COLOR HALFTONE • STRETCHED 200%

SILHOUETTE 4-COLOR HALFTONE • STRETCHED 260%

Vertical distortion

Forms that are vertically directed appear to be heavier than those that are oblique. The designer can therefore use this kind of distorted image both as a compositional device, and as a means of creating emphasis. A halftone image that has been distorted vertically creates more visual weight if it is placed at the edges of the format rather than in the center. It works as a form of visual arrest – punctuating an otherwise static layout. For this reason it is an effect that is particularly useful in youth culture magazines where every image needs to be dynamic.

Marking up

The vertical squeezing of an image is specified to the process technician in terms of percentages. Like many special effects, it is difficult to judge the results, and you may need to have some tests done.

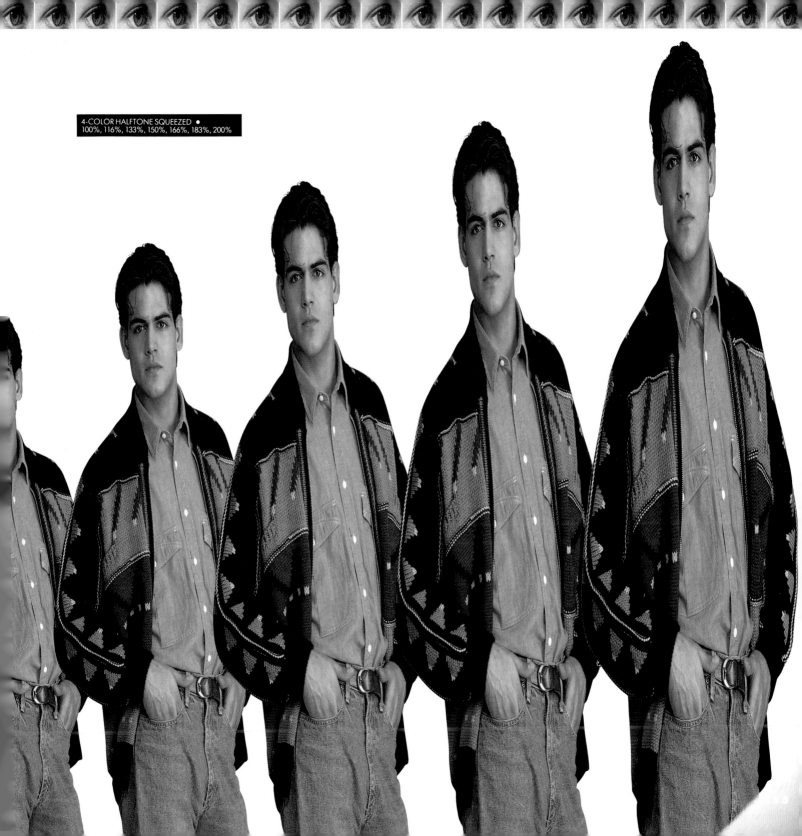

4-COLOR HALFTONE SQUEEZED ●
100%, 116%, 133%, 150%, 166%, 183%, 200%

Mezzotint

This screen effect simulates the printing qualities of gravure – early mezzotints were made by scraping the engraved plate of a solid tone from dark to light. This strongly granular quality is achieved by using a mezzotint screen. This is basically a stippled textured screen. There are many different types of patterned screens available – a mezzotint is just one of them. Although there is some loss of contrast it can be particularly effective in reproducing pencil drawings. Most creative applications therefore are usually confined to those projects that demand a chalk-like texture. The impact of objects that appear harshly mechanical can be softened by the use of a mezzotint screen. When printed in color, the screen can have a neutralizing effect in a design subject where understatement is the main theme. Mezzotint screens can be used on both black and white originals and color.

Marking up

Mezzotint screens are available in different strengths of tone and range, from fine to coarse in quality of texture. Ask the color separator to show you their range of screens with printed examples, or give them a sample to match.

BLACK & WHITE MEZZOTINT • COARSE 25%

4-COLOR MEZZOTINT • COARSE 50%

BLACK & WHITE MEZZOTINT ● COARSE 75%, PRINTED 100% CYAN + 70% BLACK

BLACK & WHITE MEZZOTINT ● FINE 50%, PRINTED 100% YELLOW + 100% MAGENTA + 50% CYAN

BLACK & WHITE MEZZOTINT ● FINE 25%, PRINTED 100% CYAN + 100% YELLOW

4-COLOR MEZZOTINT ● FINE 75%, NO BLACK FILM

Moiré

Moiré is an optical disturbance caused either by one halftone screen being out of register with another, or by the shimmering interference pattern of the subject itself. As we have previously seen, a halftone image in color or duotone is made up of colored dots overlapping each other at different screen angles. If, however, the screen angle is wrong, a visual disturbance pattern is created; fabrics, particularly silk, striped or corded material, also create a moiré effect. The problem can be alleviated to some extent by using a finer screen, but this is not always entirely satisfactory. Subjects that are prone to moiré should be excluded wherever possible. Whenever a halftone is made from previously printed matter that has already been screened, a moiré will occur when the subject is rescanned. The screen dot of the original separation clashes with the screen dot of the new separation. For this reason, previously screened material should either be avoided or shot "dot for dot." This process involves copying the same number of dots as on the original, but it can only be done if the new separation is going to be reproduced at a similar size to the original. Otherwise the screen will be either too coarse or too fine. Although moiré is normally regarded as a problem, it can sometimes be put to good creative use.

Marking up

Mark the required area clearly, asking the printer to lay the screens at the *wrong angle*. Printers spend so much time avoiding moiré that you must explain that you do indeed require a moiré pattern.

FLAT TINT MOIRE

WAVY LINE MOIRE

VERTICAL STRIPE MOIRE

OVERLAPPING CHECK MOIRE

Pixellation

Pixellation is a special effect electronically generated by computer. The on-screen image is made up of minute elements called "pixels" (short for PICtorial ELements). The image can be totally or partly constructed in the form of a grid-like pattern made up of square or rectangular patches of color. The effect is similar to a tapestry with a coarse weave, or a pointillist painting. The definition of the image is determined by both the size and number of pixels used.

There are a number of creative applications. One can, for instance, have the background section of an image pixellated, while using a normal screen for images in the foreground. Again, the pixels can be enlarged to suggest movement. The whole process of abstracting an image in this way produces a painterly quality which falls somewhere between illustration and photography. Each tiny pixel unit can be programed to deliver a wide range of colors, enabling the designer to test different color combinations. The quality of the image generated is based on the number of pixels used, the number of colors, and the memory capacity of the computer program in use. Pixellation is an effect that is sometimes used effectively on posters, where the greater the distance between the observer and the image, the better the definition.

Marking up

Pixels are always specified in size – such as 1mm × 1mm. Remember that large pixels abstract the image more than small ones.

PIXELS ● 0.5mm × 0.5mm

PIXELS ● 1.0mm × 1.0mm

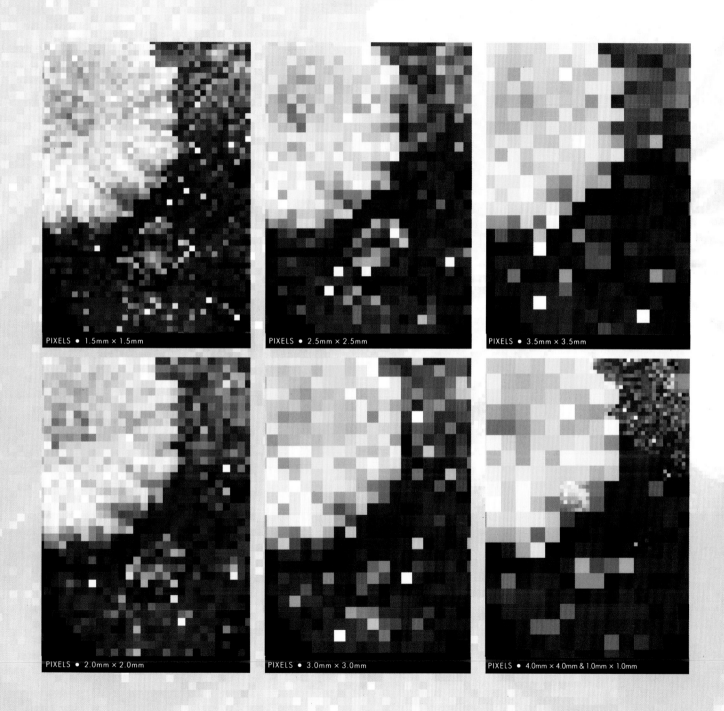

PIXELS • 1.5mm × 1.5mm

PIXELS • 2.5mm × 2.5mm

PIXELS • 3.5mm × 3.5mm

PIXELS • 2.0mm × 2.0mm

PIXELS • 3.0mm × 3.0mm

PIXELS • 4.0mm × 4.0mm & 1.0mm × 1.0mm

Photocopiers

The gradual refinement of the black and white photocopier in recent years, along with the introduction of color copiers, means that most designers now have instant access to a versatile and invaluable design tool. Apart from copying office documents, layouts, and visuals, the photocopier can also be used to produce originals suitable for reproduction.

The black and white copier can be used to produce a wide range of graphic effects and techniques. The reduction, enlargement, and distortion of type and image – the conversion of black and white copies to single color using heat-transfer films, image-reversals, and repetition – are all effects that are easily achieved. The advent of the color copier has greatly extended the range of creative applications. In the hands of a competent operator, it can be made to produce images of remarkable refinement. Much depends on getting the color balance right, and a basic understanding of color values is the key to achieving a satisfactory result. The full potential of the color copier has yet to be realized. At present, it is still in its ability to manipulate, rather than simply reproduce, that the photocopier is of greatest creative value to the designer.

Marking up

Originals should be marked up with dimensions or percentages. Colors can either be chosen from one of a standard range of "user" colors, or specified individually. However, color matching is not precise. A visit to a professional copier and a demonstration of the effects available is a good idea.

PALETTE BLACK • 100%

PALETTE PURPLE • NEGATIVE MODE, 100%

PALETTE GREEN • 100%

PALETTE MAUVE • CONDENSED 150% × 70%

PALETTE BLUE ● EXPANDED 200% × 75%

PALETTE MAGENTA ● MIRROR MODE 100%

PALETTE YELLOW-GREEN ● 1mm × 1mm PIXEL

PALETTE DARK RED ● 2mm × 2mm PIXEL

Printing line in four color

The process of reproducing a line image via the four-color set has the effect of changing an image in such a way that it can be more readily integrated with other graphic elements. It also introduces color into an image which has been supplied in black and white. The judicious use of a four-color set can greatly extend the use of line images which would otherwise be printed in black. It enables the designer to create mood and be decorative. Old wood-engravings, in particular, enlarged and printed in a pale color can be used very effectively as backgrounds, while the very use of color can add another dimension.

Marking up

You will need a four-color tint book to pick the color required. Consider the effect you want to achieve, but always be aware that if text is printing over a colored image, it needs to be legible. If you are specifying more than one tint for very fine line work, ask the color separator for a sample as registration can be a problem. The thicker the line, the easier this effect is to achieve.

50% YELLOW + 30% CYAN + 10% BLACK + 70% MAGENTA

20% YELLOW + 5% CYAN + 10% MAGENTA

40% BLACK OVER 5% YELLOW + 5% MAGENTA

40% CYAN + 20% MAGENTA + 40% YELLOW OVER 10% CYAN
+ 5% MAGENTA + 10% YELLOW

100% CYAN + 40% YELLOW

100% YELLOW + 60% MAGENTA + 10% BLACK

40% CYAN + 20% MAGENTA + 10% YELLOW OVER 5% CYAN
+ 10% MAGENTA + 10% YELLOW

Solarization

The process known as solarization is concerned with reversing, or partly reversing, the tonal values of an image by subjecting the film to gross over-exposure. The negative is exposed in the normal way. It is partly developed, then exposed to light or "fogged," before completing its photographic development. As a result, areas of shadow, which were previously un-exposed, develop as highlights. At the same time, a line of lighter density appears, along the contours which have been fogged. The reversal of negative and positive values is further compounded when colors are introduced into the image that are not normally associated with the sub-ject, and were not part of the original image.

It is an effect that came to prominence during the 1960s as part of that decade's spirit of experimentation. Psychedelic colors were most often used to imitate drug-induced hallucinations. A number of memorable posters were produced during this period which used this tech-nique, mainly for pop groups and record companies. However, a more subtle range of colors can also be used for the tone reversals to just as great effect.

Although solarization was traditionally a photo-graphic darkroom technique, it is now generally created by computer.

Marking up

This technique is by its nature unpredictable. If the solarization is being done on computer, you can sit with the operator and view the different color combinations on screen until you achieve the desired result. When specify-ing solarization, give the color separation house the range of colors you want to introduce and ask to see tests.

BLACK AND SILVER BIAS

ORANGE BIAS, NEGATIVE BACKGROUND

RED AND YELLOW BIAS

BLUE AND PURPLE BIAS

BLUE AND PURPLE BIAS, ENHANCED DETAIL

PINK AND GREEN BIAS

YELLOW BIAS, NEGATIVE BACKGROUND

BLUE AND PURPLE BIAS, FURTHER ENHANCED DETAIL

Screen effects

Halftone screens can be used either to provide a reasonably faithful reproduction of the original, or in such a way that they present an entirely different interpretation of the original.

It sometimes happens that an image reproduced with the coarsest screen – say 45 lines to the inch, provides greater visual impact than if it were reproduced using a fine screen..

Scanners can produce a variety of dot shapes, from an almost square shape, to elliptical and round dots. An enlarged square dot produces a mosaic effect similar to pixellation. The elliptical dot is more suited to subtle changes in tonal values.

Marking up

The size of dot or screen ruling is specified as the number of lines per inch or per centimeter. Choice of screen ruling depends mainly on choice of paper – but you may want the effect that a coarse screen can give.

4-COLOR HALFTONE • 40 LINES PER INCH, ROUND DOT

BLACK & WHITE HALFTONE • 40 LINES PER INCH, SQUARE DOT

4-COLOR HALFTONE • 10 LINES PER INCH

BLACK & WHITE HALFTONE • 20 LINES PER INCH

4-COLOR HALFTONE • 100 LINES PER INCH

BLACK & WHITE HALFTONE • 120 LINES PER INCH

4-COLOR HALFTONE • 30 LINES PER INCH

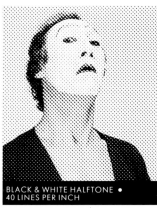

BLACK & WHITE HALFTONE • 40 LINES PER INCH

4-COLOR HALFTONE • 140 LINES PER INCH

BLACK & WHITE HALFTONE • 160 LINES PER INCH

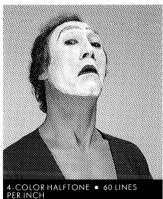

4-COLOR HALFTONE • 60 LINES PER INCH

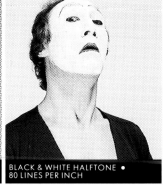

BLACK & WHITE HALFTONE • 80 LINES PER INCH

4-COLOR HALFTONE • 180 LINES PER INCH

BLACK & WHITE HALFTONE • 200 LINES PER INCH

Vignettes

The vignetting of an image is another special effect that provides the designer with an opportunity to change the pace or relieve the monotony of a page-layout made up largely of text and square halftones. A vignetted photograph is one softened at the edges in order to produce a gradual fading of the tone toward the white of the paper. Its use is usually related to the desire to provide some kind of visual flourish in the design.

Traditionally, vignettes were oval-shaped engraved illustrations, used as end-pieces in fine book production. However, vignettes can be any shape you choose. Because vignetting was originally a photographic darkroom technique, often employed when printing early portraits, it is still associated with that type of image. Vignettes can be produced by computer, electronic scanners, as part of the page make-up process, or simply by airbrushing. The visual distance between the picture at full strength and it gradually fading into white can be varied enormously.

Marking up

It is always safer to give the printer an original which you have had airbrushed, or provide him with a vignetted mask. When specifying a vignette, provide the printer with artwork for the shape you need and then give a distance over which to achieve the fade.

VIGNETTE ● 2mm (1/16in) FADE

VIGNETTE ● 4mm (1/8in) FADE

VIGNETTE ● 6mm (¼in) FADE

VIGNETTE ● 10mm (³⁄₈in) FADE

VIGNETTE ● 8mm (⁵⁄₁₆in) FADE

VIGNETTE ● 12mm (½in) FADE

Computer manipulation

Sci-tex and other such picture-manipulative computer systems are undoubtedly the most innovative development in recent years; but even with these amazing machines, the potential of a computer as a creative tool has yet to be fully realized. Sci-tex is a sophisticated electronic system that can be used for juxtaposing different images in page make-up, or for creating unique collages of images. It is possible to take several transparencies and juggle around with them — overlaying one image with another, adding special effects or placing images side by side, in a way that is not possible in any other medium. Because the original picture is stored in the computer's memory, it is easy to access the image at any time to make amendments or add new special effects.

Although originally used for stripping images together, retouching, and color-correction, Sci-tex is being used more and more creatively for manipulating images and collaging. Creating pictures on computer gives the designer an opportunity to see results on screen before producing final film and enables changes to be made easily at any time. Finally, Sci-tex generates the separated film directly and, because one is working from the original, there is no loss of quality.

Marking up

The most effective instruction is to sit with the computer operator and direct the work yourself. If this is not possible, provide clear thumbnails and a written brief of what you need; clarify all your instructions by telephone to reduce the risk of misunderstanding.

UNCHANGED SCAN

CRYSTALLIZATION

CLONING

SPOT COLOR CHANGE ON SHIRT

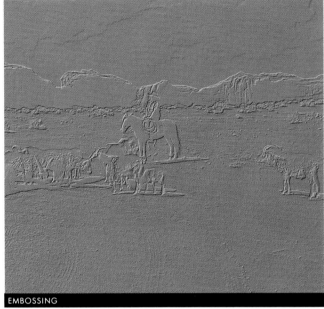

EMBOSSING

PICTURE FADE

GRADATED PIXELS

SOFT EDGE VIGNETTE

MEZZOTINT

MULTIPLE IMAGE EFFECT

POSTERIZE

COLLAGING TWO PICTURES

RETOUCHED SKY WITH LENS FLARE

TYPOGRAPHIC ADDITIONS

Country

Cowboy

MAGNIFIED SPHERE

COLLAGING TWO PICTURES

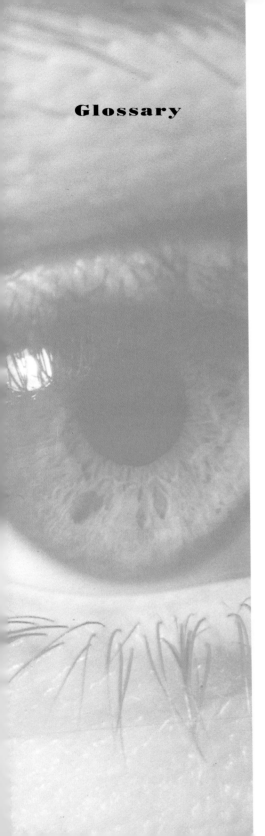

Glossary

Absorption The degree to which colors or chemicals are absorbed by paper.

Artwork Original illustrations, diagrams, photographs, and all material other than text, prepared for *reproduction*.

Assembled negative A negative made up of *line and halftone* images used in making a plate for *offset lithography*.

B

Backup When both sides of a sheet of paper have been printed it has been backed up.

Bleed When the printed image extends beyond the trim marks on a page.

Blocking out To paint out or mask out areas of the *original artwork* before *reproduction*.

Blind stamping An impression stamped into the paper without ink or foil.

C

Camera ready *Artwork* which has been prepared for *reproduction*.

Circular screen A *photomechanical screen* which can be adjusted to prevent *moiré* patterns in full-color *reproduction*.

Coated paper Paper that has been coated with

china clay to produce a hard, smooth surface.

Collotype A *photomechanical* printing process which enables a continuous tone to be printed without the use of a *halftone screen*. The printing surface is planographic, using a raised gelatin film on a glass support.

Color correction To ensure that the color values in a printed proof are correctly adjusted.

Color filters Colored sheets of glass or gelatine placed over the camera lens which, as light enters the camera, absorb or pass particular colors through. Also used in *color separation*.

Color separation The process of separating the various original colors of an image by *color filters* in an electronic *scanner*, so that the color separation film can be produced.

Contact screen A *halftone screen* which is placed in close contact with a film or plate to produce a *halftone* from a *continuous tone original*. Such screens provide better definition than the conventional glass screen.

Continuous tone Original *artwork* or photographs in which the subject reveals a continuous gradation of

tone from light to dark, before being broken up by a *dot screen*.

Copy All matter to be typeset.

Cutout A specific shape cut out of the printed sheet with a specially made steel die.

Cyan The shade or hue of blue used in a four-color set in full-color *reproduction*.

Deep-etch halftone The removal of unwanted *screen* dots by deep-etching to reveal areas of plain paper on the printed sheet.

Dot pattern The shape of individual dots — elliptical, square, or round.

Dot screen A sheet of glass or film bearing a network of lines ruled at right-angles. The screen is used to translate the subject into dots.

Drop-out/Dropped-out halftone Those parts of a *halftone negative* that have been removed by masking out.

Duotone The process in *halftone reproduction* where two *negatives* are made from the same photographic *original* using different *screen angles*. The plates made from the negatives are printed in register to produce a printed image in greater depth and detail.

 Emulsion The light-sensitive coating of a photographic film.

Erwin screen See *mezzotint screen.*

 Fifth color A color, such as silver or gold, which is sometimes used in addition to the four-color set.

Film negative A sheet of film material which has been sensitized to reveal a photographic image with reversed highlights and shadows.

Film positive A positive image on film material made as a contact from a *negative.* Film positives are used in platemaking for *offset lithography* and for photosilkscreen.

Four-color process The process of full-color printing based on the separation of images into the four printing colors — cyan, yellow, magenta, and black.

 Ghosted images The fading-out of the subject by reducing the percentage strength of the halftone dot.

Glass screens In *reproduction,* a sheet of glass with a grid of lines ruled at right angles to break up an image into *halftone* dots.

 Halftone The means by which the illusion of continuous tone is created by a pattern of dots of various sizes.

Hard dot A *halftone* dot which produces an image that is sharp and dense.

 Image area The proportion of space allowed for the total image area within a square or rectangle — even if the image is an irregular shape.

 Line conversion A means of converting an existing *halftone* image into line photographically, by eliminating the middle tones.

Lithography See *offset lithography.*

 Main exposure The first exposure in the processing of a *halftone* image.

Mark up/marking up To indicate on *artwork mechanicals,* or *copy,* instructions for *reproduction* or typesetting.

Matte finish A printing paper coated with china clay which has a non-glossy surface.

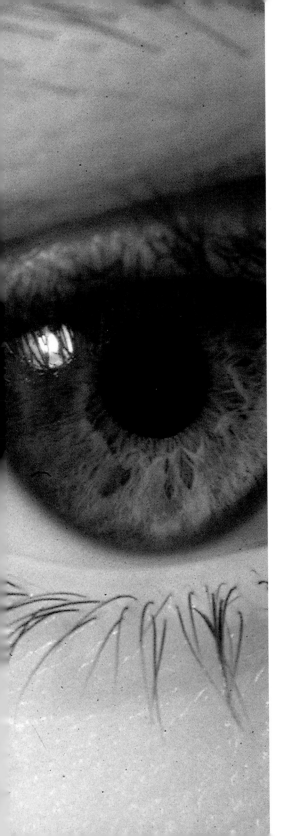

Mechanical A term used to describe *camera-ready artwork*.

Mezzotint screen A random dot-patterned *halftone screen* producing a range of tones.

Moiré A visual disturbance pattern resulting from an aberration in the *halftone* process. It can be caused by setting the *halftone screens* at incorrect angles.

 N

Negative Photographic film that has been exposed and fixed with reverse tones from which a positive image can be made.

 O

Offset lithography A planographic printing process based on the mutual antipathy of grease and water, in which the image is prepared on the plate photographically, transferred (offset) onto a cylinder and then to the chosen surface.

One-way screen A *halftone screen* which has lines ruled in one direction.

Original The original material to be used for *reproduction*.

 P

Page proofs The secondary stage in the proofing process in which pages have been paginated.

PANTONE Pantone Inc's check standard trademark for color reproduction and color reproduction materials. Each color bears a description of its formulation (in percentages) for subsequent use by the printer.

Photoengraving A *photomechanical* process for producing etched *halftone and line* printing plates.

Photomechanical Printing processes based on photochemistry.

Photosensitive Plates and film material that are chemically treated to be light-sensitive.

Pixellation An electronically generated effect in which a color image is composed of tiny square or rectangular pictorial elements known as pixels.

Press proof The proof taken before the final printing.

Process camera A specialized camera specifically used for process work in *photomechanical* printing.

Progressive proofs Separate proofs of each color used in a full-color set, as well as proofs of the full set, are produced to check tonality, color, and registration.

Proof correction marks A standardized set of signs and symbols which are understood by all those involved in design, print, and publishing.

 R

Reproduction The term in printing to describe the photographic processes used to make films from which an image is printed.

Resolution The particular quality of fine detail obtained from *photomechanical* or computer graphics.

Retouching A means of refining or altering original *artwork* with a paintbrush, airbrush, or computer system.

 S

Scanner/laser scanner A *photomechanical* instrument used in *reproduction* which electronically identifies the density of colors in an image being separated.

Screen The patterns or series of dots created in the process of making a continuous-tone picture suitable for reproduction.

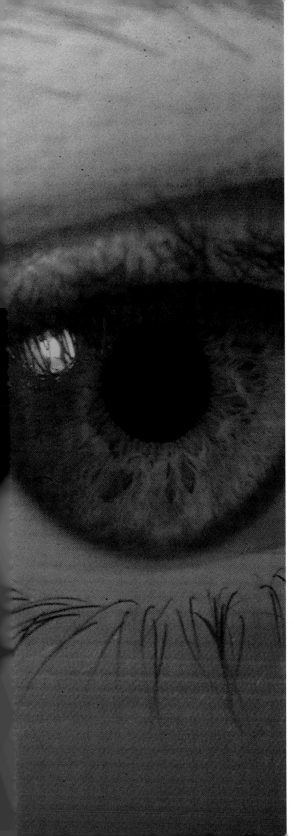

Screen angle The particular arrangement and alignment of *halftone screens* when two or more are overprinted to avoid *moiré*.

Screen ruling The ruled grid on a *contact* or *halftone screen*.

Sharpness The degree of clarity of a photographic image.

Show through A fault caused by using a paper which is insufficiently opaque, allowing the impression on one side to be visible on the other side.

Silhouette A *halftone* with background dots removed.

Soft dot A *halftone* dot using a soft emulsion which produces softer edges on the image.

Solarization A photographic process in which the image created is part negative, part positive. It is achieved by exposing the *photosensitive* material to light at a critical stage during the processing of a negative or print.

Square halftone A *halftone* image which is contained within a rectangular shape.

Stripping The assembly of two or more images to produce a composite *negative* for platemaking in *photomechanical reproduction*.

Swatch Color specimen.

Tint (1) The effect achieved in printing when a tinting medium is added to printing ink to make it more transparent. (2) The effect achieved by breaking up a solid area of tone with a *halftone* dot.

Tone line process A method of combining line and tone film images to produce line artwork.

Transparency A term which usually refers to a positive film image in full color but can also be applied to any image on a transparent film base.

Tri-tone The process in *halftone reproduction* where three *negatives* are made from the same photographic original using different *screen angles*. The plates made from the negatives are printed in register to produce an image in greater depth and detail.

Vignetted halftone A *halftone* image which is allowed to gradually fade tonally at the edge of the image.

YELLOW

At-a-glance guide to halftone effects

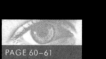

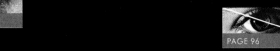

Credits

Every effort has been made to clear copyright for the pictures in this book and we do apologize if any omissions have been made.

Quarto would like to thank the following for their help with this publication. (Abbreviations used: T = top; B = bottom; L = left; R = right.)

PAGE 12 FULL PAGE: i-D Magazine. Art Director: Stephen Male at Nice

PAGE 12, INSET T: Bob Petrie/Borkys

PAGE 12, INSET B: Designed by Giant for Royal Mail Stamps

PAGE 16–17: Designed by Nice

PAGE 18, TL: Client: R. J. Reynolds. Art Director: Erik Beaton. Advertising Agency: McCann Erickson. Manipulation: Matey

PAGE 18, BL: Designed by John Warwicker and Simon Taylor at Tomato

PAGE 19, TL: i-D Magazine. Art Director: Stephen Male at Nice

PAGE 19, TR: i-D Magazine. Art Director: Stephen Male at Nice

PAGE 20, L: Designed by Sightlines for Sadlers Wells

PAGE 20, TR/BR: ZANDERS Calendar 1992 "Time.Future.Machine" from ZANDERS Feinpapiere AG, 5060 Bergisch Gladbach, Germany

PAGE 21, TL: Client: Vaux Brewery. Product: Scorpion Dry Lager. Agency: R.D.W. Advertising. Creative Director: Peter Riley. Photographer: Andrew Hayward

PAGE 21, TR: i-D Magazine. Art Director: Stephen Male at Nice

PAGE 21, BL: Designed by Sightlines for Sadlers Wells

PAGE 21, BR: Pearson Young Ltd. British Railfreight Distribution. Imaging: The Printed Picture Company

PAGE 22, T: i-D Magazine. Art Director: Stephen Male at Nice

PAGE 22, BR: Art Director: Viv Walsh. Photographer: Paul Windsor. Advertising Agency: BMPDDB Needham. Client: Crookes Health Care

PAGE 23, TL: Art Director: John Hegarty. Advertising Agency: Bartle Bogle Hegarty. Client: Shell International. Image manipulation: Matey

PAGE 23, TR: Art Director: Peter Vincent. Advertising Agency: KHBB. Client: Robinsons Soft Drinks. Copywriter: Kevin Blackmun. Photographer: Gered Mankowitz. Models: John Evans/Peter Gates Fleming. Retouching: Lifeboat

PAGE 23, B: Designed by Giant for The Crafts Council

PAGE 126–127: Visuals for singles packaging, for Blast the Human Flower by Danielle Dax. Design and art direction by Stylorouge. Photography by Simon Fowler. Image manipulation by IQ Video Graphics

PAGE 132–137: Image manipulation by Bournemouth Colour Graphics. © Heinz Steenmans/Audience Planners

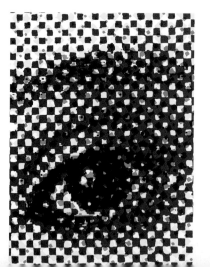